THE GENIUS OF MUHAMMAD

[Peace Be Upon Him]

ABBAS MAHMOUD AL-AKKAD

Translated by

Dr Mostafa Ali Ismail

(mostafaperth@gmail.com)

Ebook ISBN: **978-0-9953823-4-3**

Paperback ISBN: **978-0-9953823-0-5**

EXCERPT

A DAY OF HOPE

The day of the cave when Prophet Muhammad (PBUH) migrated from Mecca to Madinah [due to persecution by the tyrants in Mecca] is a day of lessons and solaces, especially during the days of anxiety, uncertainty, and anticipation. It is a day of faith, for it is a day of hope, and a day of contemplating the future by those who are not satisfied with their present and when the present world is not pleasing any of those who care about it. And when the uncertainty and anxiety prevail, be absolutely certain about one particular thing: the world is in search for a spiritual faith! No future can dwell in the hearts unless it attaches to hope and faith. In all human history, no one single great movement was driven by the past that is devoid of a look into the future. On the contrary, all great movements are built on hope in the unseen tomorrow or on goals that can be achieved in human's lifetime with something that can still be achieved in the far tomorrow...

Let them remember this those who are confused about a world drowning in its own blood, rejecting its own present, and forsaking its own future. But why are they confused? In seeking the future? In seeking faith? In seeking the reason for man's existence? Because existence alone does not justify, unless we treat humans like animals. Faith is for the future, and let us hope that the future is for faith. And let us hope that the world will always find an everlasting wisdom from the cave day and from the hero of the cave day!

The Author: Abbas Mahmoud Al-Akkad is an Egyptian thinker, journalist, poet and literary critic who was born in 1889. He received limited formal education, completing only his elementary stage. But he kept pursuing his education through personal effort to become one of the most prominent authors in the Arab world during the 20th century. His contribution to the Arabic literature was acknowledged by serving as a member in the prestigious Academy of the Arabic Language. Al-Akkad wrote more than 100 books, covering subjects on religion, philosophy and poetry. He also made a philosophical study of the Quran and various biographies of historic Muslim leaders. His most famous works are the Genius Series, “Allah”, “Sarah”, “Communism and Humanity” and “Satan”. His book “The Genius of Christ” was translated into English and some of his other books were translated into French and Persian. He wrote myriads of articles and columns in newspapers and magazines. Al-Akkad was known for his use of eloquent, flowery and complicated Arabic prose. He died in 1964.

The Translator: Dr Mostafa Ismail is a university professor and passionate translator and interpreter. He holds a professional accreditation status from the National Accreditation Authority for Interpreting and Translators in Australia (NAATI) and has been practicing translation and interpreting since the year 2000. Dr Ismail has a PhD degree in Engineering from the University of Western Australia. He was born in 1962 in Egypt before migrating to Australia in 1996, and has been living there since. Dr Ismail has delivered numerous public lectures in Australia and overseas on topics such as "Human Rights in Islam", "Relevance of Islam Today", "Scientific Miracles in Quran" and "Emotional Intelligence in Quran and Sunna".

PREFACE BY THE TRANSLATOR

ALTHOUGH THE BIOGRAPHY of Prophet Muhammad, Peace Be Upon Him (PBUH), has been the subject of many studies, books, references, and commentaries, the book written in Arabic by the Author, Abbas Mahmoud Al-Akkad, remains unique in the way it has addressed the personality of the Prophet (PBUH), producing such an elegant thesis. This book is not a mere citation of the acts and traditions of Prophet Muhammad (PBUH); rather, Al-Akkad opted to dive deeply into the traits and attributes underlying the Prophet's legacy as a manifestation of his genius, still as a human being.

According to Al-Akkad, Prophet Muhammad (PBUH) had naturally practiced all facets of genius and greatness, because he was gifted by the talents that had made him the best preacher, politician, manager, warrior, friend, and father.

The Author illustrated how the Prophet (PBUH) had such lively heart, soul, and conscience that enabled him to register the irrefutable genius in every creation around him, subtle or obvious, from the air lifting of a single grain of sand to the ever-glowing sun and moon. It was such lively elements instilled in the Prophet that prepared him for the divine call and enabled him to endure the struggle associated with receiving the 'heavy' message and delivering it successfully to all mankind. And in the way the Prophet reflected upon the genius of all creations around us is a strong message to every human being to search, ponder, and listen to the wonders of Allah's creation.

The Author succeeded in presenting Prophet Muhammad (PBUH) as a human being whose human nature made him appreciative of people's weaknesses, needs, and aspirations, while catering for these astonishingly during his delivery of the message of Islam. Al-Akkad proved how the Prophet (PBUH) persisted and persevered in his call to make it a success despite all the odds, barriers, and challenges; a message to be emulated by every individual who has goals to pursue and achieve in this life and in the hereafter.

The Author also showed that during only 23 years, the duration of Prophet Muhammad's mission, the world has changed forever; thanks to this one single man. Yet this change would have never been possible without the special qualities that were inculcated in the Prophet. It is these qualities that every person should strive to acquire and act upon, notwithstanding the divine preparation that qualified Prophet Muhammad for the most serious mission in history.

In the course of guidance and aspiration to mankind, the way the Author presented the genius traits of the Prophet (PBUH) inspires individuals to strive for nobility and justice, societies to aim for reforms and prosperity, and nations to establish and maintain order and peace.

Finally, the book shows how the Prophet (PBUH) spent all his life expending his skills, talents, and genius for the benefit of mankind, entertaining none of life's glamour; a fact that characterized all prophets before him. But in return, people will always celebrate his contribution to mankind until the end of time.

Translator: Mostafa Ismail

Perth 2016

PREFACE BY THE AUTHOR

THE READER WILL REALIZE that the title of this book: "The Genius of Muhammad" signifies the purpose of the book within its intended scope. The book is not a new [traditional] biography of the Prophet to be added to the existing, comprehensive Arabic and Western literature on the topic. For I did not mean to address the events associated with the life of the Prophet per se, although I believe there is a room for dozens of books to be written about these events and still do not do justice to the subject.

Neither is this book an explanation of Islam or some of its rulings nor is it a defense or rebuttal against claims made by rivals of Islam, since these topics have been covered by capable specialists. Rather, the book is an appreciation of the genius of Muhammad (PBUH) in proportion to what humans owe him, Muslims and non-Muslims, with the truth that instills love of the Prophet into peoples' hearts, both Muslims and non-Muslims.

For Muhammad in this context is great, because he is an example for those who wish to possess the best attributes that are sincerely wished for all mankind. He is great because he was at the most exalted standards of manners.

Appreciating the greatness of an individual should be a duty in every place and time; yet it is more dutiful in our time for two main reasons. Firstly, the world today is in much more immense need for reformers who can benefit both their own people and others; however, a reformer cannot confer guidance upon his people while he is being underestimated and experiencing negligence and ingratitude. Secondly, people have [ironically] violated the notion of greatness in our time (as much as they need it for their own inspiration), due to the fact that commonality of the public rights nowadays lured some ill-behaved people to deny the rights of those who enjoy rare qualities and need special appreciation beyond the commonality that would do them gross injustice. The notion of equality and commonality have become the norm in our modern time. This misnomer of equality has violated the rights of those great individuals in the past as much as it is doing it to those in our time. Also lured people to extend this violation is their delusion that the advances in our modern time have dwarfed and weaved everything of the past, even in the talents of souls and minds, which are actually eternal advantages that can never be weaved by the element of time.

[For example], those people think that the steam [of a machine] weaves the sail [of a boat], although the invention of the sail may reflect more ability than the steam, and without it the steam itself would have never been invented. Such critics examine the great individuals and magnates of this world preconceived that they must asperse and dishonor them, except when compelled to acknowledge their grace after they exhaust all means of injustice, calumny and vilification.

Such evil downgrades human values to 'rock bottom' and diminishes all hopes in fixing moral and psychological flaws to even below 'rock bottom'. For what would be the worth of that person who treats a great individual as worthless? And what hope in knowing the truth of something if the truth about the greatness of an individual is lost? And when a great individual is wasted in a society, expect the worst for the ordinary person.

It is for this reason that appreciation of Muhammad (PBUH), equally by Muslims and non-Muslims, in a way consistent with the understanding of the modernists is greatly useful in our time in which the criteria of appreciation have been distorted.

It is useful for humans to appreciate Muhammad (PBUH), while he actually does not need such appreciation himself. Because, in his eternal greatness, he will not be abased by a denial or harmed by an aspersion, the same way the aspersion of those who belied him during his life time expired harmlessly to him.

And it is useful for Muslims to appreciate Muhammad (PBUH) using evidences and criteria adopted by non-Muslims to strengthen that appreciation and inspire them to follow suit. And when a Muslim does this, he would be loving his prophet twice: once through his own religion and once via the general human qualities that are shared by all mankind.

Considering this book: "The Genius of Muhammad", it suffices to establish with evidence that Muhammad (PBUH) is great by all measures: he is great by the measure of religion, great by the measure of knowledge, great by the measure of emotional intelligence, and great in the eyes of those who may differ on faith but agree on noble human characters. However, humans lose [insight] when unfairness controls their hearts and drives them away from the straight truth, while the truth itself remains intact.

The accomplishments of Muhammad (PBUH) is sufficient to elevate him to the pinnacle of greatness, admiration and praise. He swayed his people from worshipping idols to believing in god. These idols were not relatively as beautiful as those in Greece to lend some admiration, even in the absence of real guidance. But they were ugly idols like those voodoos that ruin tastes and minds. So Muhammad transformed them from being worshippers of such ugliness to worshippers of the Exalted Truth [Allah]. Such is the worship of the creator of the universe, no other creator but he. [With this], Muhammad (PBUH) transformed the world from the state of stagnation to mobility, from chaos to order, and from animalistic degradation to humanistic dignity. And none before or after Muhammad (PBUH) among all reformers achieved such drastic transformation.

This accomplishment of Muhammad (PBUH) suffices to crown him the best position among the eternal elites. In fact, no one denies such achiever his due respect and can still offer it to any other human.

Yet I can go one step beyond this and state that Muhammad (PBUH) is entitled to praise for his genius, irrespective of his accomplishments. For a genius is a value in the soul before it transpires into deeds, actions and real accomplishments; genius is a value that exalts the outcomes of any assessment. And when Muhammad (PBUH) exceeds all criteria in his genius, deeds, and faith; he is then a great Prophet, a great hero, and a great man.

The hope from this book is to serve as a finger that points to this greatness of Prophet Muhammad (PBUH) in its vastness. For the finger is more capable in pointing than a full arm in embracing, and pointing to the sun can circumvent the limitations to embrace it.

Author: Abbas Mahmoud Al-Akkad

Cairo 1941

TABLE OF CONTENTS

CHAPTER 1: BIRTH SIGNS

IT WAS A COLLAPSING WORLD, on the brink of demise! The least that could be said about it is that it was a world that had lost faith as much as it had lost order, i.e. it lost the means that can bring internal and external peace; the internal peace that derives from the unseen force that spreads justice, protects the weak, penalizes the aggressor, and chooses the most and complete reforms in all affairs; and the external peace that draws from relying on a state of law to resolve disputes between aggressors and victims, to guard the road and deter the mischiefs.

Rome has just detached from faith toward a sterile argumentative culture, which became indicative of the era, while its power has diminished in land and offshore to the extent that those who used to be protected by Rome have now coveted it.

Whereas in Persia, the Persians are mocking their very religion with the throne being threatened by evil, betrayal, disorder, and temptations.

Abyssinia is lost between idols (borrowed from either civilization or barbarism) and monotheism associated with the idolism. And with this distortion in faith, it has no mission for life nor does it have an everlasting, memorable achievement.

Such world is looking forward to a different state, a world in preparation for a change or demolition before a rebuild.

A NATION

And between these faltering states is a nation that is not actually a state but in preparation to becoming a state. This is the Arab nation that has just realized its very existence and importance. It has also sensed the danger surrounding it and the shortcomings it suffers, while it is actually in control of the world commerce and business.

As when the convoys travel from the Persian Gulf to the Roman [Mediterranean] sea, they cross the desert guarded by independent Arabs under the authority or jurisdiction of none of these faltering nations. Or perhaps, those Arabs felt being under some kind of authority during the peak of the Roman and Persian power, but realized soon after that they are rather in control; when they permit, provisions exchange smoothly between the east and west and vice versa; and if they frown, those commerce veins deplete, goods diminish, and markets plummet. On the other hand, convoys travelling between Yemen and Shaam [Levant][1] or between the Red Sea and the Mediterranean are surrounded by Arab Bedouins from both ways.

It is a nation that has just awakened to its presence and realized its value among those threatening the desert, only to note clearly the abuse of those tyrannical neighbors. For Rome's Hercules sends a representative to rule Mecca; Ethiopian Abreha advances

[1] Translator: Region now including Syria, Lebanon, Jordan, Palestine and parts of Turkey

to Mecca with mighty power to destroy the Kaaba[2] and replace it with his own; and Persia transgresses both the east and south borders [of the Arabian peninsula].

That Arab nation heeded the external danger that is now inciting its awakening and attention to its very existence and also heeded the local threat that drives either toward vanishing or toward filling the grave gaps within its vitality.

Within this emerging nation is one city in which accumulates the wealth of the peninsula, and within this city a small group of elites seize that wealth.

It is a metastable state! On the one hand, you see the luxury, greed, wines, gambling, pleasure, and servitude of the weak by the stronger ones. On the other hand, you see poverty, sorrow, and doubt in reforms. But in fact, it is the doubt that investigates and disturbs not the one that submits and succumbs. For whenever wise individuals meet to discuss the faith and inner self-peace, there comes a voice among them referring to the falsehood engulfing them.

A group of people convened in Nakhla[3] to commemorate the Ozza[4] Feast when one of them said to his brethren, "By Allah, our people have no faith but falsehood, as there is no point in circling a stone [idol] that does not see, does not hear, and cannot harm

---

[2] Translator: The Sacred House in Mecca
[3] Translator: A Place
[4] Translator: One of the biggest idols in Mecca

or benefit, with that ritual blood seeping over its head. Oh people, seek another religion." They then parted ways: some of them embraced Christianity, some abandoned the idols, some retired to isolation, and some waited till the call of Islam and answered it. The one who embraced Christianity before hearing the call of Islam is Waraqa Ibn Nawfal, who was destined to hear and assure the glad tiding of the Arab Prophet. Those people dared to doubt and searched for the faith and inner peace.

Others doubted and searched for a sanction from conscience and a sanction from power. The sons of Hashem, Zohra and Taim unitedly entered a covenant under the name of Allah that they would ally with any victim of oppression to secure his rights, and this is the treaty of "Alfodoul" that Prophet Muhammad (PBUH) witnessed in his youth and referred to: "I would not love to attend better than this treaty in the house of Ibn Gadaan."

It is a state that cannot settle, but is rather seeking settlement! And it is a lively nation subject to engulfing threat from its surroundings and from within. It is a state that alarms against pending destruction; however, it is hardly possible for a nation to collapse during its awakening. It is, therefore, a state of transformation and change.

A CLAN

There is a clan within this nation, within this city, that had two branches: one group includes those with full possession of affluence and greed, with unrelenting content with the status quo, as it has ever been in line with its historical desire; whereas the other group includes those who possess piety and tolerance with intermediate traits between the strong group that transgress and possess the means for tyranny and the weak group that suffer and preserve patience with no power to resent, except to submit to the master and eat his pickings.

A HOUSE

And within this moderate branch is an honorable house that has not been plagued by wild wealth, sweeping pride, and inhumanity against the destitute. This is the house of Abdulmotalib, from the core of Quraysh and its top summit offspring, although he was not among its richest elites at the time.

The head of this house is Abdulmotalib, a man of a strong character and faith; yet he is wise despite his dispositional and faith strength, entitled to have offspring that promises and defends the faith.

Abdulmotalib vowed to slaughter one of his sons in front of Kaaba if blessed with ten of them. His people and the augury expiated him of this vow, but he refused until he was assured that his lord and his conscience were satisfied. The augury then asked them: “How much do you pay in ransom?” They said: “10 camels.” She said: “Bet to sacrifice 10 camels against the boy, and increase the number of camels by 10 each time the bet picks the boy until your lord is satisfied.” They kept increasing the number of the camels until the bet picked 100 camels. Quraysh then cheered: "Your Lord has now accepted it Oh Abdulmotalib, so release the boy."

It would have been fitter for someone who wants to extricate himself from the commitment and find an excuse to accept the offer, but Abdulmotalib insisted on repeating the trial three more times for confirmation before slaughtering the camels for people and beasts to feast.

And when the Ethiopian leader came to destroy the Kaaba, he confiscated his camels and sheep. Abdulmotalib approached Abreha asking for his camels. Abreha then responded in a politically cunning manner: "I see you are asking for your camels, but not to have the Kaaba spared." Abdulmotalib then replied wisely in confidence: "I am the lord of the camels, whereas the House has a Lord to fend it." His faith was then equal to the political manoeuvre; it was not a faith of weakness, submission or complacency.

When someone possesses such nature, conscience, faith, and leadership, it is no wonder then that he begets a prophet at a time starving for prophets and a place readier to receive him than any other place. The wonder is in fact when the outcome is the opposite.

A FATHER

And if Abdulmotalib would be a good grandfather to a noble prophet, his son Abdullah would be the best father to such a prophet. Abdullah was like a drop from the unseen sent to this life to beget a prophet and then ascend back, without sighting that Prophet.

He was a martyr in the skin of a man, to whom human hearts are attracted for the love, compassion, and mercy he enjoyed. He is Abdullah (the slave of God), the youth who was chosen for the sacrifice and the one for whom his people cried until heaven spared him, albeit for a while. And he is the young man who girls talked about his beauty and shyness. He is the one who was the target [for marriage] of hundreds of the women around him. And he is the young man who spent only three days with his bride before travelling to trade, the journey that he never returned from. He is the youth who died far from home and to him was born a noble boy while he is buried. And thus, thoughtful souls can see the chain connecting fathers of the prophets and the offspring that connects life with the hereafter and the world of the existing life with the world of death.

A MAN

It is a world looking forward to a prophet! And it is a nation looking forward to a prophet! And it is a city looking forward to a prophet! And it is a clan, a house, and two fathers who are the best fit to beget such prophet. And here he is, a man who has no match in his attributes or markers and no one can even come close to his best traits that prepared him for this most awaited spiritual mission in the city, in the peninsula, and the world.

He is of inveterate parentage, not inferior or dull to be belittled in the nation of parentages and ancestors.

He is a poor man, rather than a spoiled rich man who draws tyranny from the power of his nobleness and wealth and whose heart is clogged with the greed for might and opulence.

He is an orphan brought up among compassionate people. So he is not a spoiled child whose indulge killed in him those attributes of strive, willpower, and independence. Nor is he that neglected person in whom the cruelty killed the merit of hope, pride, natural ambitions or the virtue of compassion toward others.

And he is well acquainted with what Arabs face, living in the desert or towns. He was brought up in the desert, lived in towns, shepherded, traded, witnessed treaties and wars, and accompanied the elite but was never far from the disadvantaged.

He is then the essence of the Arabian richness in its best manner. And he is well connected with the life of his people, so that he does not behave heedlessly about it, but simultaneously he is not entirely indulged to drown in it. He is the best man from the best house for a most anticipated mission in an oblivious world.

This is Muhammad (PBUH), the son of Abdullah. He emerged when the town is in most need for him, and the peninsula is ready for his appearance! And what other signs for the awaited mission could beat these ones? And what better planning than what heaven has decreed? And what in the fables of tellers could be more astonishing than this presence and conformity?

The sign of a truthful mission is a faith a nation strives for. And it is reasons and means preparing for the very emergence of that mission. The sign is also a man who can undertake the responsibilities associated with the mission in a timely manner. When all these signs coalesce, we need not explore any other sign. And in the absence of these combined harmonious signs, no other sign would replace them nor substitute for any of the gaps.

Muhammad, the son of Abdullah, was made to be a messenger with a religion, or what else was he made for? And what achievements in life would he have made with all these introductory signs, coincidences, traits, and attributes?

Had he worked in trading all his life as he partially did, he would have been an honest, successful, and trustworthy tradesman, but trading would have only occupied a little of his traits, while the rest of his attributes would have remained idle, with no use in this particular field. And had he become the chief of his people, he would have been the one, but leadership does not do justice to his ability and preparedness.

As for what his time prepared him to face and his very nature to commit is this universal mission and nothing else. And no one in this life would have been readier than Muhammad who was made to do just this.

SIGNS OF THE MISSION

Historians exhaust their pens fiercely in an effort to track the signs of Muhammad's mission. They quote from these signs what the narrators deemed authentic or otherwise, and signs that were accepted by the trustworthy or otherwise, and signs that the actual events confirmed or otherwise, and what modern science confirmed or rejected. And historians differ in interpreting faith versus real facts and knowledge versus ignorance. But despite all of this, do they dare to differ momentarily about the traces of these signs that preceded or accompanied the birth of Muhammad (PBUH) when the call for Islam emerged and Islam prevailed? There is no lack of consensus here!

Yet none of these signs was the reason to convince anyone of the Islamic mission when the Prophet declared it, nor were these signs the reason to prove Islam itself. Because those who witnessed the claimed signs during his birth knew not about their outcomes or about the mission that will ensue after 40 years [the age of the Prophet when he received the mission]. And because those who heard and listened to the call 40 years after these signs had not witnessed any of them and did not need such means to believe in the truth they heard and needed.

Many children were born with the Prophet, east and west; therefore, if a believer relates the signs to his birth, others may argue that they are equally due to the births of others, since it took the history decades to decide between the believers and disbelievers, when the mission brought about its own proofs and signs that do not require the testimony of a believer or the denial of a disbeliever.

Yet the unmistaken, undeniable sign is that related to the universe and history. The universe events said that life was in need for Muhammad, and the history facts said that Muhammad was the holder of this mission. And there is no other word after the sign of the universe and history!

CHAPTER 2: THE GENIUS OF THE PREACHER

THE WORLD CONDITIONS had then agreed to an awaited mission. And the circumstances of Muhammad nominated him for that mission. But it was possible that both world conditions and Muhammad's circumstances matched, but without the means needed to deliver the message in the best way.

It was quite possible for the world to anticipate a prophet who never emerges, and it was quite possible for a prophet to emerge in a suitable house and environment, but without the qualities needed to deliver the message.

Yet what occurred harmoniously in Muhammad's mission is the wonder of the wonders and a miracle above all miracles, since despite the gravity of that mission, its size, diversity of its phases and the harmony among them, it was all of the kind that can readily be accepted by the mind without compulsion or urge. For Muhammad possessed the attributes necessary to succeed in every great mission of the history.

He had the eloquent tongue and language. He had the power to bring hearts together and gain trust. He had the power of faith in his call and his eagerness to make it a success. And these are the attributes of the Prophet, which are different from the circumstances around him; yet they are the pillars needed for delivering the message, even when all the circumstances are in accord.

THE ELOQUENCE

Eloquence applies to speech, how to utter words, and the contents of these words. For it is possible that the speech could be eloquent but uttered with no eloquence. Or it could be that the wording and saying are both eloquent, but the content lacks the eloquence that seeps into ears and hearts.

But Muhammad's eloquence was complete in his words, the way he talked, and in what he said. He was the most Arab among the Arabs, as he said, (PBUH): "I am from Quraysh [i.e. the heart of Arabs] and was breastfed in Banu Saad Ibn Bakr [the most fluent Arab clan]." Accordingly, he was the most eloquent Arab with this Quraysh, Bedouins upbringing, and that is indeed the eloquence of speech.

But a man could be Arab, from Quraysh, and breastfed in Banu Saad Ibn Bakr, but his pronunciation is incorrect, or with a disliked voice, or with uncoordinated wording in such a way that he could have the eloquent wording but not the articulate pronunciation. However, Muhammad enjoyed beauty in his eloquent utterance as well as in his wording. And the best who referred to this is Aishah [his wife], when she said: "The Prophet (PBUH) used not to talk the way you do, but rather in clear distinctive words that are memorable by a listener." And narrations agreed in the absence of faults and mistakes in his letters and articulation of sound and agreed in his ability to place his words in the most coordinated manner, for he used to speak well with strong logic.

A man could be an Arab from Quraysh, breastfed in Banu Saad, with sound wording and pronunciation, yet he lacks the substance that warrants a listener. The Prophet was, too, free from voidance of substance in his integral eloquence. No one single speech was authentically narrated from him but serves as an evidence that he indeed was given words which are concise but comprehensive in meaning, and that he was blessed in what he says as much as in how he says it.

HANDSOMENESS AND CONFIDENCE

Along with his eloquence, Prophet Muhammad (PBUH) enjoyed both handsomeness and disposition that made him appeal to whoever sees him and made him attract hearts of his acquaintances, and this is a quality that neither a friend nor an enemy argues about it. None in this life reached this quality of Muhammad (PBUH), both among the weak and rich individuals.

And it suffices when we talk about the love he received from the weak ones what happened with a young slave man who lost his father – Zaid Ibn Harithah. His father showed up after a long time, but still, this young man preferred to stay with Muhammad (PBUH) over being united with his father. Another case is when Maisara, the servant of Khadija [Prophet's first wife] introduced Muhammad to his lady with a promise of profit and success for his trading style, although Maisara was in much more need to promote himself with what he praised Muhammad with.

On the other hand, it suffices when we talk about the love Muhammad received from the strong ones that he gained love and respect from people of different attitudes and traits such as Abu Bakr, Umar, Othman, Khalid and Abu Obaida, who they were all great people.

A man can be likeable, handsome with excellent deposition, yet with no much share of trust or confidence in him from his circle because being a likeable man is different from being a trustworthy one. And it is quite possible that the two qualities coexist or do not coexist since they are not necessarily conjoined. But as for Muhammad, he gathered both love and trust as they can ever possibly and harmoniously coexist. And he was well known for his honesty and trustworthiness as much as he was well known for his handsomeness and kindness. And both his very enemies and opponents testified to his honesty and integrity as much as those who loved him did.

He was fully acquainted with the status he possessed among his people, and he was keen to use this for their guidance and making them desirous of his call; so he would ask them: "If I tell you that on the other side of this hill there is a huge army ready to attack you, will you believe my word?" And they would say: "Yes, we have never accused you of a lie." Yet man hates what shocks his belief and legacy, even when he sees the truth supported by a thousand proofs. For the people did not belie Muhammad and neither did they deny him honor nor honesty, but they hated to believe him the same way someone hates to believe true news that he finds it bad for what he likes or for those whom he likes, while he is in fact absolutely aware of the truth before him.

FAITH AND EAGERNESS

However, it is a fact that despite the numerous harmonious circumstances and the rarity of the attributes above, there is still a quality the preacher needs more than his need for eloquence and handsomeness; that is his belief in his own call and his eagerness for it to succeed. For numerous preachers succeeded without eloquence, fluency or prettiness, but none succeeded without believing in what he preached and having the eagerness to proclaim it.

Muhammad (PBUH) spent his youth denouncing both the wrongness and the idols of his time. And he was joined in this belief by people who were less than him in nobility, sensitivity, and rejection of abomination. They believed, like him, in the evil of both the time and people and in their need for a religion different from worshipping idols and manners different from those of the time. And for Muhammad to surpass them in this urge, it is because this complies with his nature and the legacy he had from his father and grandfather.

And when he believed in his own mission, and he was called by his lord to undertake it, he did not jump on this faith over an hour or a day, and he did not hasten the matter as someone who would deceive himself before he deceives others. Instead, he hesitated until he became certain and he worried until he was assured; and when the revelation was delayed for a while, he even thought that his lord had abandoned and forsaken him and did not accept him to deliver the message, until he got assurance from his lord's revelation and the faith of his heart and his companions. He then declared his message with his conscience being satisfied and assured in the manner prophets and pious people before him did, despite the difference between him and them in terms of rank and preparedness and the difference between his time and theirs in the type of reforms needed.

It is no wonder then that Muhammad is the owner of the mission, and it is not surprising for his mission to follow its course and achieve its goals. In fact, the surprise is those who ignore this fact today driven by the desire of their hearts like those who rejected it yesterday and deliberately covered the light of the mission by their own hands.

SUCCESS OF THE CALL

No grand movement in history can be clearly understood as much as the call of Muhammad, thanks to the straight, clear reasons that can be uniquely explained. And there is nothing that can distract someone from this clear, natural reasons, except a twisted, delusive desire to claim that the Islamic call was an extra thing unnecessary in this life and that the success of the call is unreal and driven only by threats and promises or by sword and temptations of paradise pleasure, wine pleasure, and the pleasure of female companions with beautiful, big and lustrous eyes.

What terrorism and what sword! When a man fights those around him, he fights in hundreds and thousands, but those hundreds and thousands who entered the new religion were subjected to swords of the polytheists but did not raise a sword. And they were subjected to distress and did not reciprocate, and they were driven out of their homes to save themselves and their children from the cunning and venom of the spiteful folks and did not reciprocate.

They did not embrace Islam by the sword of the single unarmed Prophet while surrounded by the spiteful folks. But, on the contrary, they embraced Islam despite the swords of the polytheists and the menace of the strong and controlling folks. And it was only after they had increased in numbers and supported each other that they carried swords to resist the evil and stop terrorism and threat against them. They did not take the swords to commence aggression or overpower people because the Prophet did not entirely initiate all the wars he entered, whereas all his wars were defensive and protective.

On the other hand, regarding temptations of paradise pleasure, wine pleasure, and the pleasure of female companions with beautiful, big and lustrous eyes, if this was a reason for the belief, it would have been more likely for the wicked, lewd, and rich self-indulged polytheists to accept the call, and it would have been more likely for the Quraysh tyrants to be the first to prolong life and retain the blessing. For pleasure after death is desirable for the luxurious as much as it is desirable for the deprived, and it could even be more desirable and closer for the former and they may be even more keen and desirous to have it, because deprivation after luxury is more difficult than the opposite for someone who never tasted or experienced a change.

Abu Lahab[5] was not disinterested in luxury than Umar[6] was. And those who rushed to Muhammad were not more desirous of the pleasure than those retracted. But when we examine the two parties, we find one clear central difference between them, that is the difference between the good and evil, the merciful just and the arrogant transgressor, and those who minded and listened to the word of truth and those who stood arrogantly and rejected the word. This is the clear difference between those who rushed [to accept Islam] and those who stayed behind, while it is not the difference between the one who seeks pleasure and the one who

---

5 Translator: Uncle and enemy of Prophet Muhammad

6 Translator: A companion of Prophet Muhammad

forsakes it, or between someone deceived by lavishness and someone who was not deceived by lavishness.

It may be clear to call the fact above from the example of Umar in how he embraced Islam, since his story is exemplary in answering the call of Muhammad, which refutes every claim about the threat and temptations as being factors in persuading the strong or the weak. Ibn Isaaq narrated that: "Umar went one day and drew his sword and set out to kill the Holy Prophet (PBUH) and about 40 of his companions who gathered in a house near Al-Safa, men and women, including his Uncle Hamza, Abu Bakr Al-Siddiq, Ali Ibn Abi Taleb among other Muslim men who stayed with the Prophet and did not migrate to Ethiopia. On the way, he met Naim Ibn Abdullah who asked him: "Whom are you after Umar?" He said: "I am after that renouncer Muhammad who divided Quraysh and ridiculed its wisest and insulted its deities to kill him." Naim said: "You are fooling yourself Umar. Do you think that the sons of Abd Manaf[7] will let you live after you have killed Muhammad? You better first set your own house in order." Umar said: "Who in my family?" Naim said: "Your brother-in-law Said Ibn Zaid Ibn Amro and your sister Fatima Bent Al-Khattab; they both have accepted and followed Muhammad."

[7] Translator: Clan of Prophet Muhammad

Umar then turned his steps to his sister and brother in law. While Khabbab[8] was with them somewhere in the house, Fatima took the manuscript and hid it under her thigh after Umar already heard Khabbab reciting while approaching the house. When he entered, he asked: "What are these voices that I have heard?" They replied: "Nothing." He said: "By Allah, I have heard and I am told you have followed Muhammad." And he slapped his brother in law Said Ibn Zaid. His sister then tried to push him away from her husband, but Umar smacked her and cracked her head bleeding. When he saw his sister's blood, he regretted and backed off. And he said to his sister: "Show me this manuscript that I heard you reading to see what Muhammad has come up with," and Umar was a literate. His sister replied: "We fear you about it." But he said: "Do not." And he swore by his gods that he would give it back to her after reading it. Umar's sister turned hopeful that he may accept Islam when he said so. And she said: "My brother, you are impure by your disbelief, and this should not be touched except by the pure." So Umar went for a shower, picked the manuscript that had the Chapter of Taha. And when he read part of it, he said: "How beautiful and noble this saying is!" When Khabbab heard this, he said: "Oh Umar, I wish that Allah has chosen you in answering the supplication of his Messenger when he said: "Oh Allah strengthen Islam by either

---

[8] Translator: Companion of Prophet Muhammad

Ibn Al-Hakam Ibn Hesham or Umar Ibn Al-Khattab, Allah Oh Umar."

Umar then said: "Direct me to Muhammad to accept Islam." And Khabbab said: "He is in a house at Al-Safa with some of his companions." Umar then pulled his sword and rushed to Prophet Muhammad (PBUH) and he knocked at the door. When they heard him, one of the companions checked from a hole in the door and saw him holding the sword. He spooked and said: "Oh Prophet of Allah, this is Umar holding his sword." Hamza said: "We let him in, and if he is here for good we do so, but if he is here for evil we kill him by his sword." And the Prophet said: "Let him in." And when the man did, the Prophet rushed to Umar and grasped his cloth close to the neck and pulled him firmly saying: "What brought you son of Al-Khattab? By Allah, you are not going to stop until Allah brings down his wrath upon you." Umar said: "I came to believe in Allah, his messenger and what Allah has revealed." The Prophet then made Takbeer[9] so that his host knew that Umar had accepted Islam. The companions left the house afterwards feeling stronger when Umar accepted Islam right after Hamza, knowing that they will support the Prophet and retaliate from their enemy."

This is how Umar accepted Islam, and this is the position of his story from both temptation and threat. He went to kill Muhammad by his sword, but no Muslim targeted him by a

---

[9] Translator: saying "Allah is Great"

sword. And he recited a part of the Chapter Taha that has no mention of wine or pleasure; that is: "*Ta, Ha. We have not sent down to you the Quran that you be distressed. But only as a reminder for those who fear [Allah]. A revelation from He who created the earth and highest heavens, The Most Merciful [who is] above the Throne established. To Him belongs what is in the heavens and what is on the earth and what is between them and what is under the soil. And if you speak aloud - then indeed, He knows the secret and what is [even] more hidden - Quran, 20:1-7.*"

There is no fear then nor is there temptation in the way Umar accepted Islam; rather, it is mercy, repentance, and regret.

And there was no fear or temptation for those who accepted Islam while less than Umar in power and strength, because by doing so, they exposed themselves to the sword rather than submitting others to the act of a sword when they believed in Allah and his Messenger. And those who rejected did not do so by virtue of abstention or bravery such that one would say that those who rushed to Islam did so by virtue of the opposite [i.e. desire to pleasure and fear of the confronting power]; rather, the two parties differed when the situation warranted righteousness and straightness. So, whoever was closer to these traits, whether rich or poor or enslaved, accepted it, whereas the deviant one rejected it. And this is the criterion between the two parties before a sword was ever raised to fend Islam and before a sword was ever raised to scare off insulting swords.

And no one would dare to classify the two parties in such a way that someone like Abu Bakr, Umar, and Othman are categorized under the reasons of fear and temptations while those tyrants from Quraysh are categorized under the reasons of impeccability and bravery, unless whoever judges shares the prejudice of the disbelievers from Quraysh in the form of persistence and denial. The call of Islam did not succeed, except that it was much sought by the era and was very well introduced by the events, and the preacher who held it was well prepared both by his lord and by the fitness of his circumstances and attributes.

Accordingly, there was no need for this call to have something miraculous that might have been rejected by the human mind or to have an eccentric justification for the desirous person to maneuver with. For the call is absolutely clear for the one who wishes to understand, and it is the most straightforward thing for the one who wants to be straight.

CHAPTER 3: MUHAMMAD'S MILITARY GENIUS

We said in the previous chapter that Islam did not succeed because it is a religion of war as its enemies resonate, but it succeeded because it is a much needed religion undertaken by a successful preacher. And among the means of its success, there is nothing difficult to understand within this merit.

In this chapter, we want to iterate that despite Muhammad's avoidance of wars, he used to excel in war arts better than his aggressors, and that he did not avoid attacks or initiation of wars because of inability or fear of what he lacked or did not perfect. Instead, he avoided wars because he considered it as an abhorred, inevitable necessity, with no other means to avoid it. And when possible, he would avoid it once there is a way to achieve this.

And before elaborating, we have to recall some of the facts that show the difference between Islam and other religions regarding wars. This is to prove that like all other religions, Islam's position is to avoid violence and that it would have never triumphed with violence alone without being entitled to triumph, and that other religions would have never avoided any of the actions of the Prophet had their calls been the same and their reasons like his reasons.

The first fact is that the criticism of those who say that Islam is a war religion could be believed, if any, in the beginning of the Islamic era as discussed before, when many polytheist Arabs embraced it, and without them, Islam would have never had soldiers or carried a sword.

But the reality is that in its beginning, Islam used to be the victim of aggression, while it did not initiate aggression to anyone. And this position remained even after people had accepted the call, as they used to fight those who initiated fighting, and no more: "*And fight in the Way of Allah those who fight you, but transgress not the limits. Truly, Allah likes not the transgressors – Quran, 2:190.*" Muslims preserved patience until they were instructed to fight the aggressors all as they are waging war on all of them. So, Muslims did not launch aggression or compulsion. And as indicated earlier, the wars entered by the Prophet (PBUH) were entirely defensive, and none was initiated, except as a defensively pre-emptive act after ensuring that the enemies broke the covenant and insisted on fighting. And this applies to his wars against Quraysh, the Jews or the Romans. For example, in the Battle of Tabouk[10], the Muslim army returned peacefully after realizing that the Romans had abandoned fighting in this particular year. And it was the news that the Prophet gathered that indicated that the Romans were mobilizing their army along the Arab borders; so when they

[10] Translator: A battle that did not eventuate between Muslims and Romans during the life of the Prophet (PBUH)

had retreated, the Muslim army also retreated despite the effort, hardship, and cost spent on the preparation.

And the second fact is that Islam would be rightly blameworthy if it fought with a sword an ideology that could have been otherwise fought with evidence and persuasion. Accordingly, Islam is not to be blamed when it fights with the sword a stumbling power that blocks its way and prevents access to those who are willing to listen, since power cannot be displaced except by power, and this cannot be achieved but via force.[11]

The masters of Quraysh did not present themselves with any ideology that opposed Islam. All they had was a legacy of dominance and traditions that they deemed necessary to maintain this dominance, generation after generation. And the excuse they clung to in this regard is that they inherited these traditions from their forefathers and that termination of this dominance terminates with it the power and the status they had.

Moreover, the Prophet in his call targeted those great kings and princes of nations, because they are the ones that would oppose new faiths. And it was shown by many facts that it is the power that blocks the way of Islam not the ideas of the intellect nor dogmas of the elders. Suppressing the resistance of those

[11] Translator: While Islam never compels people to accept it, it is essential that people must have safe access to the message before they decide whether to accept it or reject it. This philosophy surrounds the concept of Jihad in Islam.

influential men and kings would have removed the obstacles facing Islam, making the use of force unnecessary.

And it has been clear from recent and ancient historical practices that power is inevitable to achieve the goals of the reformers and those who seek transformation. This can be seen in the experience of France in the 19th century, Russia in the 20th century, and Mustafa Ataturk in Turkey [20th century], as well as other similar cases in other countries.

Fighting a power with a force is different from fighting an idea with a force, and the difference between the two has to be distinguished because they are indeed very different.

And the third fact is that Islam did not resort to the sword, except in cases all legislations would agree to. For example, how can a state react to those who revolt against it from within, if not by resorting to the weapon? And this is what Quran decided, saying: "*And fight them on until there is no more tumult or oppression, and there prevail justice and faith in Allah; but if they cease, let there be no hostility, except to those who practice oppression – Quran 2:193.*" So when some people in a state carry weapons against other fellow citizens, what other than the power of force could be used to stop them? And this is what Quran exactly instructed: "*If two parties of believers fight, reform between them. If either of them is insolent against the other, fight the insolent one till they revert to the order of Allah. If they revert, reform between them with justice, and weigh with justice. Allah loves those who weigh with justice – Quran, 49:9.*"

In both of the cases above, weapon is the last resort, and once the insolence is over, dependence on the weapon ceases, followed by reforms and unity or by the act of acceptance and choice.

And the fourth fact is that there are central differences among divine religions that have to be considered in this regard. For Judaism or Israelism, as the name suggests, was confined within the children of Israel more than being an open call for all people to embrace. So their children disliked the religion being shared with others the same way members of the same family hate to be joined by others. For this reason, they did not trigger their tongues, let alone raising swords to proclaim Judaism and get others to join. Therefore, there is no point in comparing Islam with Judaism in this regard.

On the other hand, Christianity was first concerned with manners and ethics more than being concerned with dealings and state affairs. Christianity then appeared in states already possessing protective laws for dealings and state affairs [to protect the state] the same way fortified priests protect a religion. As such, Christianity did not impose laws for dealings or constitutions for this reason, not because dealings and constitutions are not parts of the religion per se. Afterwards, Christianity was embraced by countries ruled by powerful states [that already have their laws and rules].

But Islam appeared in a free region subjected to none of these foreign forces, and its appearance was to reform life, fix dealings among people, and establish security and order. Otherwise, there was no point in its propagation among Arabs and beyond.

Accordingly, it is natural and logic that Islam differs from Christianity in the way they both emerge, independent of humans' input. And the proof of this point is that Christianity did like Islam when states and armies were established and when Christians defected foreign rulers, and wars among Christian sects surpassed all initial Islam's wars combined.

And the other [fifth] fact is that Islam legislated Jihad[12] and that the Prophet (PBUH) said: "I have been commanded to fight against the people till they testify La ilaha illa Allah (There is no true god except Allah) and if they do this, then their blood and property are secured except by the rights of Islam, and their accountability is left to Allah."[13] And Quran says: "*So fight, [Oh Muhammad], in the cause of Allah; you are not held responsible except for yourself. And encourage the believers [to join you] that perhaps Allah will restrain the [military] might of those who disbelieve. And Allah is greater in might and stronger in [exemplary] punishment - Quran, 4:84.*" And indeed Muslims conquered lands outside their borders, and they did not do this,

---

[12] Translator: Jihad in its vast meaning in Islam is to struggle in the cause of Allah

[13] Translator: This statement does not negate that there is no compulsion in embracing Islam

and would not have been able to, expect by weapons. But these conquests were late in time, well after the full establishment of the state of Islam. Therefore, it cannot be claimed that it was a means to propagate Islam, since Islam had already spread well before then and established full control in its land and recruited soldiers that believed in it and were ready to die for its cause[14].

And these conquests were necessary for the security of the state before being necessary to proclaim the call. So, if we assume that the Muslim Calif [ruler] did not have a religion to proclaim, it would still have been imperative that he secures his state against the chaos emanating from Persia and Rome and stops the evil leaking through his own sanctuary. Furthermore, Islam permitted conquered nations to keep their religions and pay tax and obedience to the ruling government. And this is the least a victorious could ask of a defeated.

Moreover, comparison between the status of the world before and after Islam reveals that the position of Islam was one of persuasion for those who can be persuaded because [after Islam] peace actually prevailed among people and it was never the case, and relationships among nations normalized, and it was never the case. [With Islam] people felt assured regarding their lives, wealth, and honor, which were all exposed freely to any aggressor who possessed power and status.

---

14 Translator: Late wars in Islam were to lift oppression and allow people to choose their faith freely

And if someone says that those who were called to Islam were not convinced in the beginning, the answer is that this does not negate the fact that they became convinced afterwards. Indeed Islam is persuasive to those who choose and choose well, as much as it is powerful to compel those who block its way toward reform.

When one examines the mental evidence, he would not find a difference between someone who wins you by providing food and medicine and someone who wins you because you fear the wrath of the ruler. For the witness that you feed and clothe to support you in a court is no different from the witness that sees the whip in your hand to obey you in that exact court. Both do not employ mental persuasion or strength of evidences nor do they defend a belief based on knowledge or insight.

The summary of the discussion above then is that Islam did not initiate fighting, except when confronted, which is justified by other legislations and all rights. And those who were faced by the sword of Islam would have been also faced by swords of other religions, except if we deny Islam the right to carry the weapon or refute its need to call for its cause, ignoring that Islam is both faith and order. Accordingly, Islam is no different from any other state that mandates people to support the order and rejects revolt.

THE INSIGHTFUL LEADER

Islam was not a religion of war then! And the Prophet was not a man of war whenever there was a way to avoid it. Yet he was the best insightful leader when the war is inevitably dictated by necessity. He knew the arts of wars by revelation better than anyone else who knew it by study and practice. And he used to be squarely right in choosing the time to mobilize his army and drawing his plan in a manner that brings success and accuracy, while embracing the virtue of mutual consultation with his companions. In fact, accepting advice is a sign of good leadership, hand in hand with signs of creativity and achievements because a good leadership is the one who benefits from the talent of every expert, the same way it benefits from the bravery of the courageous soldiers. Undoubtedly, such virtue [of inviting others' advice] recruits all powers of opinions, hearts, and physical strength.

The Battle of Badr was the first exposure of Prophet Muhammad (PBUH) in leading a big war. He did not disregard to take the advice of Al-Habbab Ibn Monzer when he suggested that the Muslim army must relocate its first position.

Prophet Muhammad (PBUH) comprehended from this single experience of the Battle of Badr more ever than dedicated war commanders can understand from multiple wars, such that if a highly competent war critic examines his tactics, he will find it difficult to change a thing or advise a critique. And in this regard, we choose Napoléon Bonaparte to prove the innovation in the Prophet's war tactics, by showing the analogy with such great war general.

1. Napoléon used to focus in his battles on eradicating the enemy's military power as swiftly as possibly; he was not interested in striking cities or ambushing stations. Rather, his utmost concern was directed to launch a strike, surprising in most cases, against the enemy's protective army with a swift attack, confident that a win in such attack will substitute for any other attempt that may be otherwise suggested by others. And in doing this, Napoléon used to benefit from three main issues: [1] to choose the most suitable site, [2] to seize the opportunity, and [3] to surprise the enemy before full preparation. However, the Prophet had adopted all these tactics in their fuller details well before Napoléon. As indicated earlier, Prophet Muhammad (PBUH) never commenced an aggression, but once he realizes that an enemy is on the move, he would not spare a respite as much as he possibly could. On the contrary, he may get the news of an imminent attack, like in the Battle of Tabouk, during harsh conditions of drought, a scorching weather, and hardships; but even with these circumstances, he is not deterred from following the tactics he developed. And he never relaxed over a swift preparation for this battle, including urging Muslims to donate money and recruits

soldiers, regardless of the rumors made by the hypocrites expecting a grand defeat of Muhammad's army, which did not happen. And he used to target the military power to undermine the morale of the enemy and its supporters by such initiative. The exception was when his enemy took the initiative but later paid a hefty price, as in the case of the Battle of Combined Forces [Al-Ahzab or the Battle of The Ditch).

2. And Napoléon used to say that the morale power is worth 3 times the power of numbers. Indeed the Prophet (PBUH) used to rely greatly on this morale power, which in essence is the power of faith [in case of Islam]. The ratio above may have reached five folds in some of the Prophet's battles, despite the superiority of the enemy in weapons and vehicles besides its superiority in numbers. The miracle of faith here is much superior to any advantage Napoléon had by morally inciting his men in terms of patience and determination. For the Prophet fought Arabs with Arabs, Quraysh people with Quraysh people, Arab clans with Arab clans; therefore, it cannot be claimed that there was any physiological advantage to any party over the other, as in the case of Napoléon's armies. All the superiority here [in favour of Prophet Muhammad (PBUH)] is actually referenced to the faith and belief.
3. Along with his tactics to eradicate opposing military power, Napoléon never neglected to destroy the financial

and commercial powers of his enemies. For example, he used to fight the British by preventing their commerce and ships from arriving in Europe, forcing them to go through France instead of England. This is how the Prophet fought Quraysh in its business, sending his platoons successively when he learnt about a travelling convoy for the enemy. But some of the fanatic writers from Europe denounced this tactic and called it robberies, while it is actually the exact act of confiscation that the international law concurred, and was actually adopted by army generals at all times; and we witnessed it during World War I and II in a rational manner in some cases and in excessiveness and foolishness in other cases.

4. We indicated earlier that Napoléon used to focus his attention on the enemy's army with no interest in invading cities or getting concerned by besieging his enemy unless for imminent necessity. And when we analyze the battles of the Prophet (PBUH), we realize that he did not besiege a place, except when it is the only means to combat the force that may be behind, before full preparation or before committing betrayal and plotting, as he did in his siege of Banu Qurayzah and Banu Qaynoqaa[15]. The assault in these cases was akin to launching an initiative attack in a chosen battlefield, with no much of a difference.

[15] Translator: Two Jew tribes in Madinah

5. Napoléon was known to be very proud of his own military capabilities, especially in his war tactics, but despite this very strong pride, he never relinquished consulting his peers before launching a war or building the intention to. Despite his intelligence and wisdom, Muhammad (PBUH) used to consult his companions regarding his war tactics and defense plans and accept their advice in the best manner. And what was discussed above about the opinion of Al-Habbab Ibn Monzer [in the Battle of Badr] is an example when he advised the Prophet to relocate the Muslim army, malfunctioning all water wells in the area, except one for Muslims to use, such that the enemy could not access it. Plus, there are many narrations that the Prophet accepted the advice of Salman Al-Faresi to excavate a ditch [in the Battle of the Combined Forces] on the borders of Madinah at the spot that could be accessed by the enemy. That ditch was indeed excavated, and the Prophet worked in it with his own honorable hands. Accepting Salman's advice was indeed an act of a wise leader in accordance with the traditions of great leaders. Yet we believe that even in the absence of Salman's advice, the Prophet would have advised of the same [i.e. excavating the ditch], since he was extremely attentive to closing breaches and protecting his back in all of his war encounters. And in the Battle of Uhod [the second battle of the Prophet against Quraysh], he protected his back by

the mountain and installed on it some 50 throwers to prevent the enemy from penetrating and besieging the Muslim army. He instructed the throwers: "Protect our backs, as we are concerned the enemy may attack us from behind. Maintain your position and never abandon it. If you see us defeating them and seizing their army, never move from your position. And if you see us killed, do not support us. All your task is to shoot their horses with your arrows, since horses do not advance when thrown."

The leader who cares about a gap on a mountain would not neglect to address a gap in the city. Yet it is the mutual consultation here that is meant to invoke the analogy between what the Prophet had done and what Napoléon excelled at. Therefore, it is [such mutual consultation] a quality in great leaders that does not take from their reputation in developing tactics and devising means.

6. No one was known to care for reconnoitering and interpretation [of intelligence information] as much as Napoléon did. But the insight of Prophet Muhammad in this regards was indeed exemplary. When he saw his companions beating the two slaves [belonging to Quraysh] watering from the well of Badr, because these slaves mentioned the army of Quraysh not the convoy of

Abu Sufyan[16], he knew with his rightful insight that the boys were truthful and were not deceptive. He asked the two slaves about the number of the enemy's army, but they did not know. He then enquired about the number of camels they slaughter every day. He used this information to estimate the power of the enemy by knowing how much they eat. And he (PBUH) used to rely on the right people in his keenness to reconnoitre, using those who are best acquainted with the roads and routes. Plus, he had the habit of holding what we call today 'the defense council' before commencing a war to hear from every expert or interrogate evidences gathered from reconnoitre.

7. Napoléon used to be very cautious against tongues and pens, saying that he would fear from four pens what he would not fear from 10,000 swords.

But the Prophet (PBUH) was the best to realize the impact of propaganda in winning wars and achieving goals. This is why he used to punish and eradicate those individuals who broke conventions, defamed Islam, incited the tribes to fight him, and insulted him and his religion harshly. He combated this by sending his platoons to fight the transgressors in their shelters.

---

[16] Translator: Muslims left Madinah assuming that the mission was just to raid a commercial convoy that belonged to Quraysh and led by Abu Sufyan. But unbeknownst to them, Abu Sufyan fled, leaving Muslims to face Quraysh's army in the Battle of Badr.

And for this, Prophet Muhammad was blamed by some of the prejudiced European writers and was likened to Napoléon when he kidnapped Duke Dungan and also what was said about his attempt to kidnap the English Poet, Coleridge, who used to slander Napoléon while attracting ears to his magical poem. Yet the difference between the two cases is significant, for the war of Islam was a mission and a belief; in its essence, it was a contention between monotheism and polytheism or between godhood and idolism. As such, confronting an army with an army was only one facet of this contention.

Accordingly, it will not be a state of peace then when someone fights the core of Muhammad's message and targets him by attacking the heart of his Islamic mission, even if that person does not mobilise people to fight or incite to break a treaty. For that person, despite that, is actually fighting in the very actual field of war and should expect his enemy to deal with him as a fighter, especially with the war being everlasting and did not stop for a while, except to resume.

But in the case of Napoléon, the war between him and his enemies was that of armies and weaponry. Accordingly, he was not entitled to kill someone who did not confront him with a weapon or was not convicted by a law of execution. Additionally, Napoléon never undertook the

> responsibility of proclaiming or refuting a religion. And it would have been futile if the Prophet of Islam compromised with those who fight his very religion, even if they do not confront him with a sword, for it is less concerning to be tackled by a sword than being tackled in the heart of his mission, which was indeed being targeted.

This is a general comparison between the tactics and traditions that Muhammad (PBUH) had developed first and was later adopted by Napoléon after centuries. In this regard, it is incumbent that we judge the leadership by the value of the idea or the tactic before we judge it by the size of the army or the type of weapons [i.e. when we compare between Muhammad and Napoléon on war issues].

Muhammad did not adopt war as a trade. And he did not use it, as mentioned above, except to combat an aggression or fend against animosity. Thus, if despite this, he perfected the art of the wars he had to launch, he had then excelled over that mighty leader of late wars [Napoléon] who learned it, lived it, and was never isolated from it since his youth until residing in his exile, without achieving some of what the illiterate leader [Prophet Muhammad] had achieved in the desert.

The Prophet also excelled in employing reconnoitre as he excelled in mobilizing fighters, in that his way of choosing the place and purpose as well as the leader and providing him with advice and support was an exemplary for all times, especially the modern time where intelligence has improved dramatically and spying techniques have become complicated. For example, it is common in modern wars to hear about sealed commands issued to leaders of platoons and warships that must be opened in a specific place or after certain time or in the middle of the sea at a particular longitude and latitude, etc. And in these cases, it is possible that only the leader may be aware of the details of the mission while his men are oblivious to the destination and whether it is a battle or just a reconnoitre maneuvering until only a few hours before the mission when the detailed instructions are recited to all for preparation and action, with no fear of disclosure at this stage for the difficulty facing the enemy to prepare within that short period, especially if it is a marine move. The issue of these sealed instructions is not new and was a prophetic practice in its best form. The example here is when he sent a book with Abdullah Ibn Gahsh and commanded him not to open it until he had been for two days on the road. The content of the book was: "Move until you reach Batn Nakhla [place] in the name of Allah and his blessings. Do not force any of your companions to join you and continue with your followers to Batn Nakhla and watch for the convoy of Quraysh and bring their news."

This is an example of the sealed commands that are comprehensive in every aspect, considering the past or the present, especially considering the beginning of religions. Firstly, by following this tactic, the Prophet concealed the issue from those around him, in case one of Quraysh's spies is present, or one with a good intention discloses it without knowing the consequences and danger of his act. For it is likely that among those around him were companions that were weak or disobedient. Seeking to accomplish businesses through secretiveness was a wise tradition of the Prophet (PBUH) in all of his endeavors, which is much more incumbent to follow at the time of wars. This is why he used to conceal his real intention by intelligently referring to a destination different from the one he actually targets, a tactic followed by war leaders nowadays.

And the two observations that could be noted from the book of the Prophet to Abdullah Ibn Gahsh is: [1] to conceal the mission from his companions and [2] not to compel anyone to pursue the mission after reading the commands, and this is the most important observation in this regard. For a man can be forced to fight because he fears death if he flees, but for sure he cannot undertake a successful reconnoitring mission under compulsion. The outcome could in fact be quite the opposite if someone is coerced to undertake such tasks, with a possibility that he may lie about the news or receive the intelligence carelessly, or even disclose the secrets of his oblivious companions to the enemy. And this is why states struggle tremendously to watch spies by spying on the spies and examining every piece of intelligence time and again to ensure its authenticity before deemed reliable.

In World War II, a new experiment was made for those who advance and undertake the task of gathering intelligence. Hitler was known to rely on individuals from his army who land from warplanes behind the opposing army to sneak to transportation stations and isolated villages to cause confusion, havoc, and corruption and transpire a false impression that the whole army is nearby to suppress morale and resistance of the enemy. Those advance guard used to carry communication equipment to contact their seniors remotely. This tactic of Hitler was admired by many and denounced by many.

The reason for admiring Hitler's tactic is that it was successful in disconnecting communication and fostering rumors and confusion within the enemy's camp, plus it was new in its form, although it was not new in terms of goals and objectives.

And the reason for the criticism is that every benefit from this tactic relied on the faith and intention [of those who undertook it]. A mission of that nature entails that the leader of the advance guard must have eagerness and enthusiasm to accomplish it without being watched by his seniors, as it is easy for him, being sole, to surrender to the enemy if he could not accomplish his mission in the assigned spot, to save his life. And this will not eventually lead to any punishment from his own camp. In this case he will find lots of excuses to offer if interrogated and questioned. In situations like this, collection of convicting evidence is impossible in the noise of two or more camps.

This tactic of Hitler would be inevitably a failure unless executed by uncompelled, fanatic followers who never doubt their missions. It is for this reason that such tactic relies on having volunteers who share moral brotherhood and belief rather than being the achievement of mainstream tactics that traditional soldiers are trained for. Evidently, if not that the Nazis spent about 10 years before World War II inciting hatred and deep patriotism and creating hostility in their youths to remove the need for supervision and control, such tactic of Hitler would have dramatically failed with the worst consequences.

And this point clearly illustrates the wisdom of Prophet Muhammad (PBUH) in making voluntary acceptance of a reconnoitre mission a prerequisite for embarking on the mission since coercion in this case would never yield any successful accomplishment.

Secondly, it is a reconnoitre mission that would not avail if executed by a compelled, coerced person, where the most critical quality is his faith, good intention, and love to the commander. And if that person lacks this quality, he then lacks everything.

As for the purpose of the whole task of the intelligence gathering, the Prophet was well aware of its benefits and extremely keen to get it accomplished, prudently realizing that an unknown enemy is like an enemy sheltered by a castle, but in this case protected by the unacquaintance that could preclude the right preparedness with the right means at the right time, and hence deny the victory.

And while writing these chapters, the Russian war reminds us how Napoléon was hit in that field when his intelligence was first hit. Again, it reminds us how this same mistake was repeated in the way Hitler is invading Russia the same way Napoléon invaded Russia yesterday.

In the case of Napoléon, one of the reasons for his defeat was ignoring the advice offered by some of his confidants in the war council before his incursion into Russia, for his false belief that the Russian Cesar will ask for peace.

Among the reasons for Napoléon's defeat is that the Russians used to retreat before his advance in the dark and evacuate the cities and roads so that he cannot find someone to ask about the position of the retreating army or pick from his answers something that can be gathered later by intelligence; the element that he relied on heavily.

But as for Hitler, he was tackled from these two weaknesses the same way Napoléon was hit, although the latter was expected to be more vigilant and careful. It was known that Hitler was at odds with his generals, as they knew about the Russians much more than he did. And it is known that he made mistakes in the intelligence gathered about the enemy when he assumed that the Russian public is on the brink of revolution and awaiting his raid to support the invader regardless of who he was, even when it comes from a Slavonic opponent, not a German Proponent.

Muhammad (PBUH) did not study what Hitler and Napoléon studied, but he never committed such mistake in any of his battles. And we may be able to understand when we study his eventful and everlasting exemplary era that such a study is as useful as studying recent eras and contemporary war generals.

The platoon of Abdullah Ibn Gahsh should not be put behind before we give justice to all of its military issues because it contains several aspects of the prophetic traditions and Islamic legislation in this regard. For it was an intelligence gathering platoon, and this platoon was never commanded or permitted to engage in fighting. Nevertheless, after opening the sealed instructions, two people of this platoon were searching for their camel when taken prisoners by Quraysh. These are Saad Ibn Aby Waqqas and Utba Ibn Ghazwan. The rest of the platoon then camped by a tree when a convoy belonging to Quraysh carrying its trade and led by Amro Ibn Al-Hadramy passed by; it was the last days of the month of Rajab[17]. At that time, Quraysh had already confiscated the wealth of some Muslims, including those belonging to some men in that platoon. The band then consulted as to whether they should fight the convoy, but could not reach a resolution: if they let off the convoy, it will seek refuge by the

---

[17] Translator: The month of Rajab was a sacred month in which launching a war was forbidden

sanctuary of Kaaba, losing the opportunity to make for what Quraysh had seized from them before; whereas if they fight the convoy, it would be a breach of the sacred months [forbidden for war]. Yet they went ahead to fight and injured a few people and killed the leader of the convoy, Amro Ibn Al-Hadramy, by an arrow. They also took two people prisoners. When they returned to Madinah, they offered a share of the booty to Prophet Muhammad, but he refused to take it and said: "I did not command you to fight during the sacred month." Other Muslims blamed them for disobeying the instructions of the Prophet, and the band received an overall cold reception in Madinah.

Quraysh seized the opportunity and started to incite other Arabs, and some of the Jews got involved stealthily and echoed that Muhammad and his companions are profaning blood and wealth during the sacred month. On the other hand, Muslims said it was actually the month of Shaban [non-sacred]. And then the following Quranic verses were revealed: "*They ask you concerning the sacred month about fighting in it. say: fighting in it is a grave matter, and hindering (men) from Allah's way and denying him, and (hindering men from) the sacred mosque and turning its people out of it, are still graver with Allah, and persecution is graver than slaughter; and they will not cease fighting with you until they turn you back from your religion, if they can – Quran 2: 217.*" After this revelation, the Prophet seized the convoy and the two prisoners. Quraysh wanted to ransom-free them, but the Prophet requested: "Not until you free our two companions, as we fear for their safety being with you. You kill them, we kill yours."

This is the story of the platoon and the issue of disobeying the Prophet's orders and the laws that followed. Yet if we were to write it today using modern terms, how would we? It is undoubtedly an event of an advance guard or borders: a state sends some advance guards to its borders for intelligence gathering or patrolling, only to engage in a fight with the advance guard of another state, unbeknownst to the two governments. What happens in this case is that the other government considers the accident to be a one off that does not warrant launching a war. And that government accepts that the perpetrators will be punished by their own government, and the issue is then resolved. Alternatively, the other government may insist on compensation, which will resolve the matter if accepted by the accused government. Otherwise, there will be a further negotiation, bargaining or finally a war.

The above would be the case if the two parties consider the case to be both casual and a one off, and none of them or both consider it a case that warrants legislation on how to react against as a mainstream event, or document what they would accept or reject of the relating provisions and rules.

However, Quraysh did not consider the event of the platoon as a one off, but did not declare the war, as it concealed the intention for a war before that event. But Quraysh actually raised the issue of legislation for fighting in the sacred month. It was, therefore, incumbent on Islam to state clearly the legislation of such events, which actually was the case.

There is no doubt that Abdullah Ibn Gahsh indeed disobeyed the commands of the Prophet, and there is no need to investigate this further. Yet the real issue is the following: what is the verdict now regarding fighting in the sacred months? And how much rights do the polytheists have in taking refuge in the sacred months, while they pay no heed to the Muslims sacredness and are still fighting them and driving them out of their religion as much as they possibly can? And what would the answer be to the defamatory campaign launched by Quraysh concerning the sacred months that Quraysh itself does not respect?

This is the resolution that Islam had to declare. And as it did, it followed the way of modern legislations in its military conflicts and still being used today. For there are sanctities that if violated by a state it renders its own sanctities exposed for others to violate or being punished for justice and compensation for damages and losses. Otherwise, sanctities will just serve to shield the aggressors rather than being a deterrent and blocker to the aggression, as they are supposed to be.

And today, any aversion of war between two states can lead to a relationship cut, with anticipated consequences of mutual confiscation of each states' assets and taking opposite nationals as prisoners. It would still be acceptable to use the confiscated assets to compensate for the damage the state or its national incur, and use the prisoners as hostages to be treated in a manner similar to its own nationals on the other side.

This is what happened exactly following the platoon of Abdullah Ibn Gahsh, which is precisely the act of the approved international law: two prisoners against two prisoners, and the money of the convoy against the assets seized by Quraysh. There is no justification here for the noise made by the fanatic, missionary critics regarding this familiar event or the resolution reached by the Prophet and Islam about it. For those critics ignore the circumstances and forget that the contemporary international rules in our time have not offered a judgement that is more wholesome or wiser than that condoned by the Prophet and revealed by the Quran in connection with such event. And in fact it is equally a two-way resolution, for and against Muslims, in such a way that a fanatic would be confounded if he tries to replace it [i.e. the Islamic resolution] by something more practical and acceptable.

And this inspired leader [the Prophet] was an expert in recruiting for the advance guards and intelligence teams as much as he was an expert in mobilizing every power he had when the war was inevitable, be it the power of opinion, the power of tongue, or the power of influence. In fact, we are not aware of someone who employed the power for a call in a successful and fruitful manner as he did (PBUH).

A WAR HAS TWO OBJECTIVES

As known, a call for war has two primary objectives among many others. The first is to convince your opponent and others of your rights, and this objective is well covered by Quran, prophetic sayings, and Muslim preachers, since the whole religion revolves around rights. And the second is to weaken the will of your opponent and instill division within its supporters so that you abate their urge to fight. And in this, the Prophet achieved with one single man what states equipped with disciplined troops, offices, headquarters, and money could not achieve.

[In relation to the Battle of the Ditch, or the Combined Forces][18], Ibn Isaaq narrated (with rephrasing) that Nuaym Ibn Masud came to the Prophet (PBUH) [during the Battle] and said: "Oh Prophet of Allah, I have accepted Islam, but my people are not aware of this. Command me therefore to do whatever you desire." The Prophet said: "You are one person, but go to those people [the enemy] and try to instill division among them, for indeed war is deception."

Nuaym went to Banu Qurayzah [the Jews in Madinah]. He was a close friend of the tribe. And he said: "Oh Banu Qurayzah, you have known my love for you and my sincerity in advising you." And they agreed. He said: "Quraysh and Ghatafan have their own

---

[18] Translator: In this battle, the clans from Quraysh, Ghatafan and other Arab clans launched war against Muslims by invading Madinah. Although there was a treaty in place between the Jews of Madinah (Banu Qurayzah) and Muslims to defend the city, Banu Qurayzah allied with the enemy against Muslims.

interests in this war, which are different from your interests. This is your city, you have your wealth, your children, and your womenfolk here, and it is not in your power to flee and take refuge in another city. On the other hand, Quraysh and Ghatafan have their land, their wealth, their children and their womenfolk away from this city. They came to fight Muhammad. They urged you to break the treaty you had with him and to help them against him. So you responded positively to them. If they were to be victorious in their encounter with him, they would reap the booty. But if they fail to subdue him, they would return to their country safe and sound, leaving you to him and he would be in a position to exact the bitterest revenge on you. You know very well that you would have no power to confront him. You should not join forces with them until you take a group of their prominent men as hostages. In that way, you could carry on the fight against Muhammad either till victory or till the last of your men or theirs perish." They responded: "You have advised well."

Nuaym then left and went to Abu Sufyan Ibn Harb, Quraysh's leader, and spoke to him and other Quraysh leaders. He said: "You know my affection for you and my animosity to Muhammad. I have heard some news, and I thought it is my duty to disclose it to you, but you should keep it confidential and do not attribute it to me." They agreed. Nuaym continued: "Banu Qurayzah now regret that they have decided to participate in the hostilities against Muhammad. They have sent a message to Muhammad saying: "We are sorry for what we have done, and we are determined to return to the treaty and a state of peace with you. Would it please you then if we take several Quraysh and Ghatafan nobles and surrender them to you? We will then join you in fighting them - the Quraysh and the Ghatafan - until you finish them off." "Muhammad has sent back a reply to them saying he agrees. If therefore the Jews send a delegation to you demanding hostages from among your men do not hand over a single person to them. And do not mention a word of what I said to you."

Nuaym then went to his own people, Ghatafan, and spoke to them in a similar vein. He gave them the same warning against expected treachery from Banu Qurayzah.

On the night of Saturday, the 5th of Shawwal, Abu Sufyan wanted to test Banu Qurayzah; so he sent Ikremah Ibn Abu Jahl with others from Quraysh and Ghatafan. They said: "Our siege of Muhammad and his companions has been a protracted affair, and we have become weary. We are now determined to fight Muhammad and finish him off. So join us in the battle with Muhammad tomorrow." "But tomorrow is Saturday, and we do not work at all on Saturdays," said the Jews of Banu Qurayzah. "Moreover, we would not fight with you until you hand over to us seventy of your nobles as hostages. We fear that if the fighting becomes too intense, you would hasten back home and leave us alone to Muhammad. You know that we have no power to resist him." Upon Ikremah's return, Quraysh and Ghatafan replied that: "We are not going to give you a single man of ours. So come out to fight tomorrow if you will ever do." When Banu Qurayzah heard this, they said: "Masud was right about what he said. Those people want you to fight and if they find the opportunity they will seize it. Otherwise, they will go back to their own places and leave you confronting Muhammad."

And then Allah instilled division among them and sent down on Quraysh and their allies a fierce and bitterly cold wind, which swept their tents and their vessels away, extinguished their fires, and destroyed their structures. Quraysh and Ghatafan then fled to their homes. And the Prophet went back from the ditch to Madinah. This was the call of Nuaym Ibn Masud.

No one-man mission had the success of such man. And there is no match in seizing the opportunity of the natural factors and the constituents of the enemy to this case. For every word said to any of the factions was the right word at the right time, and this is indeed the weakening and tearing mission in its best.

UNMATCHED LEADER

In holding a comparison between old and contemporary battles, it is prudent to consider the concept of the 'leadership' before we look into the shape or the size of the battle. For if we look at the latter, the comparison would be futile, since it is unquestionable that one million people in the battlefield [as in today's wars] is way greater than 10,000 [as in the old days of the Prophet], and a war that is managed via radio and phone is more wondrous than the one controlled by voice and hand signals; the canon is more destructive than the sword and the bullet is more fatal than the arrow. Therefore, there is no point in holding a superficial comparison that will lead to a known outcome, in that modern wars are so huge that they dwarf ancient leadership in comparison. But when we consider the thinking of the leader, we may realize that guiding and directing a thousand men could be more skilful than guiding and directing a million on vehicles or on foot, and among them those who ride the most sophisticated machines.

It is exactly this point that allows us to realize that Muhammad (PBUH) was the best, unmatched leader of his time in the way he thought and in the way he used to benefit from his companions' advices, plus it shows us his rare ability in mobilizing the powers of mind, weaponry, and words. And this is a testimony for a messenger derived from the testimony for a leader adept in war arts. For whoever has this effective and successful tool but still uses it only inevitably and for necessary defensive purposes is the messenger who is driven by his divine message rather than his military leadership, since he does not employ it unless dictated by the message of guidance.

And what adds to this testimony is that the person who avoids unnecessary fighting is a non-fearing and brave, but not like in the case of some of the reformer guides who could be of a good character more than being of a brave character to the extent they avoid fighting, as they do not perfect it.

Some orientalists claim that the Prophet contributed in the Fojjar[19] war by preparing arrows, and this act of him is close to his character rather than being able to engage courageously into the heart of the battle, as if they meant to say that he was unable to do anything more critical. And this is an error in the way these orientalists understand this great soul that enjoyed a multitude of traits summed in both the best of compassion and the best of bravery and nerve. For Muhammad was in the forefront of his army when wars intensified and feared by the most courageous men. Ali Ibn Abi Taleb used to say: "When the battle flared, we used to seek shelter in the Prophet of Allah so that no one would be nearer to the enemy than him."

For example, had it not been for his steadfastness in the battle of Hunain when most of his army fled and he was solely facing the enemy's throwers and stabbers, it would have been a definitive defeat for Muslims. And had it not been for his noble bravery and nothing else, why would he opt for a swift move into the streets of Madinah under the darkness of the night to explore the safety of the city when raids and siege threatened it? Madinah, at the time, was jammed by people who would have taken care of this task while the Prophet is in the comfort of his house, but he

---

[19] Translator: This is a war among Arabs that was launched before the time of prophethood

wanted to assure himself without being swayed by fear, so he did not assign the task to anyone else.

And his participation in other battles was that of a leader who does not exempt himself by virtue of the leadership from sharing the rest of the soldiers what they normally face. It is the type of bravery that does not hide at a chance, although it may have the right and acceptable excuse.

Yet when the leader is well versed with wars, capable to steer them, unfearful of what they bear, but he then opt to indulge in the bear minimum that he absolutely needs, he is then the messenger who derives this entitlement from his military leadership, and the one who further derives his beautiful attributes from being a messenger.

CHARACTERISTICS OF GREATNESS

Yet greatness has marvelous characteristics, though for known reasons, let alone the greatness that reaches such level [i.e. of Muhammad].

Among these characteristics is [that the great person] may possess two contrasting features concurrently, because it [the greatness] is intrinsically multifaceted, so that it can be interpreted differently by different people, or could be seen from two different angles by the same looker at two different times.

And because greatness may invite extreme love or extreme hatred, with a room for moderation, it may be difficult to be sighted or explained by everyone, even with good intention. However, with ill intention and delusive desires, aberration is not very unlikely.

Among the characteristics of the greatness of Muhammad (PBUH) is that he was described to have different attributes by the fanatic opponents of his religion. As for some of them, he was of softness that would prevent him from committing to wars, while for others, he was of obduracy that drives him to kill and shed human blood unjustifiably. Yet Muhammad was of neither of these two facets.

For if his bravery refutes the element of weakness implied in the softness and denounced fear, his whole life since his childhood negates the accusation of obduracy and harshness. For he was in all his relationships with his family, his nurses, his wives and his servants, an exemplary in terms of the mercy that was not even possessed by prophets.

There is no point in spending time discussing the cases listed by the prejudiced who tried to prove the bloodshed in the peninsula, as most of the narrated cases were never irrefutably proven, especially the story of the Prophet incitement to kill Asma'a Bent Marwaan, the Jewish woman, because she used to satirize Islam and Muslims. In such cases, the Prophet in a clear instruction prohibited killing women and repeated this on more than one occasion, to the extent that some of the [Muslim] scholars prohibited killing women, even if they engage in the battlefield, unless for otherwise preventing an inevitable danger.

The only case that warrants consideration is the death of Kaab Ibn Al-Ashraf[20] who used to insult Muslims, defame them, instigate their enemies, conspire to kill the Prophet and engage in every plot to undermine Islam, although he and his people Banu Al-Nadir[21] entered an alliance treaty with Muslims to maintain peace within Madinah and fight against their enemies, and to adopt kindness and cooperation when treating each other.

But Ibn Al-Ashraf knocked down the treaty and incited the enemies against Muhammad and his companions; and while in Madinah, he insulted and abused the wives of the Prophet and committed slanderous lies against them in a manner that would otherwise be abhorred by any nobleman or ardent Arab.

Regarding his story, it is narrated that the group [of Muslims] that went to kill him arrived at his fortress and called upon him, and he was a recent groom at the time. He descended quickly to meet the group, but his wife warned him: "You are a fighter, and a fighter does not leave his fortress at the hour of the night." And indeed the wife said the truth when she referred to him as being a fighter. Such fighter must then be dealt with as the one who lied in his oath, as he did not honor his covenant, he did not have

---

[20] Translator: A knight and poet Jew who showed and acted with animosity toward Islam

[21] Translator: A Jew clan in Madinah

a conscience or tribe values to deter him, and he was untrustworthy regarding Muslims while in his fortress. As such, he was not entitled to be granted amnesty.

It was narrated that the Prophet approved the assassination of Ibn Al-Ashraf, and this has been condemned by some of the European historians, as they considered it to be a violation of war laws and an act similar to what Napoléon did when he kidnapped Duke Dungan and trialed him unjustifiably, despite the great difference between the two cases as discussed above.

However, we can summarize the issue here by pointing to modern international laws regarding acts similar to the sins of Ibn Al-Ashraf, though with much less gravity in infidelity, betrayal, and attack of honors. The international laws state that a prisoner of war must honor his pledge not to resume fighting and entail that his government never assigns him duties that would expose him to trials in which he will not be entitled to be treated any longer as a prisoner of war after carrying a weapon against those who released him first time or against their alliances. And in this case, he will justifiably be trailed as a criminal and get executed.

Modern laws then punish to death for a crime that is much less in magnitude than what Ibn Al-Ashraf actually did, as he did not only betray Muslims but also conspired, incited, and stained honors.

And there is no context for questioning elements of mercy or cruelty in applying such law when we recall the underlying reasons that necessitate and impose requital on citizens of the same nation, let alone war circumstances between enemies.

PRISONERS OF THE BATTLE OF BADR

In addition to the controversial issue of Ibn Al-Ashraf, some orientalists blame the killing of some of the prisoners of the Battle of Badr and the move that the Prophet took to watch the victims of the battle and spoils after the war had ended. This is a case that has to be correctly examined with consideration of the context and personnel. For it is not related to the general rules that Islam established regarding wars and prisoners of wars in the general sense; but in actuality, it is the case of certain individuals that tortured Muslims and punished them severely in a reckless and indifferent manner. Neither is it the case of ordinary prisoners that were recruited for the first time with no history of shameful acts. The reality is that killing those particular prisoners was not a random act, but a requital against torturers who fell into the hands of the defeaters. This is accepted by every law, and it is expected that a punishment must inflict the defeated individuals who committed crimes beyond the normal acts of wars and what goes with them. A difference exists between those particular prisoners and the one who is just a soldier in the field who bears no hatred to you prior to or after the war, and in his deeds, there is no reason for questioning or revenging after he accomplishes his duties in an honorable war.

As for watching the killed individuals in the battlefield, apparently those critics forgot that satisfaction of the triumphant by his victory is a natural human act that does not warrant critique, unless the motivation is just to celebrate the blood, and this was never claimed by any of the witnesses of the act of the Prophet or slandered by either a Muslim or a polytheist.

Also the critics of the Prophet forgot that there is a difference between the man of modern time watching blood and a man watching blood in the old Bedouin wars and the general lives of Bedouins, in reference to the lives of those shepherds in which blood is shed on a daily basis and reference to the lives of clans that were used to invade or get invaded frequently.

You do not accuse a surgeon of cruelty because he got used to seeing dead and bloodied bodies and wounds. Otherwise, medicine cannot be a mercy for life unless surgeons are used to filling their eyes of these scenes courageously, whereas you accuse someone of cruelty when he sees such scenes but does not react shockingly. On the other hand, no such man lived in the desert and attended one of its battles who gets shocked in the battlefield by something he had not seen before, and no one in this case can accuse him of cruelty and joy in watching blood.

The story would have been different had these critics witnessed the Battle of Bader by themselves to see, by the eyes of the

Prophet, the ramifications of this battle as being the most decisive that had changed the face of Islamic history. They would have seen, by the eyes of the Prophet, two armies: one in a huge number in both personnel and weaponry, and the other is one-third in number with almost no weapons, except mere swords and with virtually no ride, except their own feet. And those critics must have felt the concern of the Prophet over the consequences of this battle and listened to him supplicating to his lord: "God this is Quraysh. It has come with all its arrogance and boastfulness, trying to discredit the Apostle. God, I ask you the victory you promised. God, if this Muslim band will perish today, you shall not be worshipped." And those critics must have seen him stretching his arms staring at heaven and focused in his prayers until his garment fell off his shoulders while Abu Bakr was calling him: "Ease yourself, for your lord will fulfil what he promised you", while he is unaware that his garment has fallen, and his companion is calling upon him, because he was focused on his supplication.

And they [the critics] must have known how keen Quraysh was to leave some people behind to return to Mecca during or just before the battle to continue the contention against the Prophet and repeat the confrontation so that he would give up and realize that he cannot persevere any longer, and indeed perseverance in such situations is hard to exercise.

It was incumbent on the critics to know all of the above to understand that the feeling of satisfaction [by the Prophet] in such critical circumstances is not at all strange, but rather it is a natural feeling of a lively soul that reacts to its life surroundings in situations of both peace and war. The first thing that comes naturally and faithfully to a lively soul in such situation [i.e. victory in the Battle of Badr] is satisfaction, a change from distress to joy, a check on the dead ones from Quraysh and others who returned back unharmed readying for a repeat, and an examination of those spoils of war that had almost enticed some of the fighters, as it was their first encounter with no Quranic revelation yet about spoils or prizes.

Muhammad was indeed a lively, impassioned man rather than a feeble hermit isolated in his hermitage, suppressing every motive or emotion. Therefore, it was unlikely, and against the intuition of a fighter, to expect a leader like him to ignore examining the outcomes of the battle that invoked all such concern and could have dire consequences. For he was, from the very moment after his triumph, entitled to comprehend his victory, what could have happened next, and what a small band could do to a large band, to extrapolate for possible subsequent confrontations. And we have today those military press reporters who study similar encounters and find it dutiful to stay behind after battle cessation to explain the lessons of victory and defeat and document that essential information expected for all wars. In fact, Muhammad's immediate departure from Badr [i.e. without examining the outcomes] would have been a strange act that does not fit his status as a leader who must study and benefit from every lesson.

AFTER THE BATTLE OF AL-AHZAB [THE COMBINED FORCES]

While we are talking about mercy and cruelty, it is useful to examine what the European historians criticized in this regard, especially (in addition to what was discussed above) execution of the fighters from Banu Qurayzah after the Battle of The Combined Forces. Those historians treat the execution as an appalling act and consider it a violation of war rules. But they ignore critical points that must be invoked vividly before expressing any judgement on this case.

These critical points include the facts that Banu Qurayzah broke their covenants many times, making holding any new treaty with them futile. They also accepted the ruling of Saad Ibn Muaaz[22] whom they chose, and Saad followed the Torah in his ruling, the book they believe in, which reads: *"When you march up to attack a city, make its people an offer of peace. If they accept and open their gates, all the people in it shall be subject to forced labor and shall work for you. If they refuse to make peace and they engage you in battle, lay siege to that city. When the Lord your God delivers it into your hand, put to the sword all the men in it. As for the women, the children, the livestock, and everything*

[22] Translator: A companion of the Prophet who later died in the aftermath of the Battle of The Combined Forces. He was an ally of the Jews.

else in the city, you may take these as plunder for yourselves. And you may use the plunder the Lord your God gives you from your enemies – Deuteronomy, 20:10-15)."

The critics must ask themselves after this: what could have happened to Muslims if defeated by the combined forces? Consequently, the ruling of Prophet Muhammad in the case of Banu Qurayzah is deemed fair, wise, and correct. For no one can be entrusted with the fate of a nation and its protection against betrayal and extreme hostility of its enemy and desecration by its rivals more than once and still does not follow the ruling of the Prophet. The fact is that one campaign in the modern time launched by an armed band against armless people defending their homes and rights involves cruelty and torture that significantly outweighs the punishment that Banu Qurayzah received plus all other wars between the Prophet (PBUH) and his rivals and enemies of his religion, recalling that they always surpassed him in numbers, wealth, and weaponry.

Muhammad's military leadership genius is approved by war techniques and arts, ethics, God's and people's rules, and rational individuals from his followers or enemies sides.

CHAPTER 4: MUHAMMAD'S POLITICAL GENIUS

PROPHET'S POLICY WITH RIVALS AND FOLLOWERS

POLITICS HAS SEVERAL MEANINGS in the modern literature. It can cover the relationships and protocols among states, including treaties and secretarial arrangements. It also covers relationships between the ruler and his nationals. Or it could be among parties and ministries in terms of programs and calls. And each of these relationships has its own meaning and nomenclature in the modern norms, even when the terminology 'politics' lumps all together.

The Prophet (PBUH) engaged in many of the acts that fall under 'politics'. Yet among all of his political activities, the most conspicuous, comprehensive, and distinctive over his military leadership, public admonition, and all of his other qualities is the 'Treaty of Al-Hudaybiyah'[23], from the moment he called for Hajj (pilgrimage) to the time when Quraysh breached the treaty.

The way Muhammad (PBUH) managed the treaty of Al-Hudaybiyah revealed clearly the way he managed policies with his rivals and followers and how he relied on peace and

---

[23] Translator: The Treaty of Al-Hudaybiyah was held between Muslims and Quraysh when Muslims wanted to perform Pilgrimage to Mecca but were denied access. This event occurred after the third battle between Muslims and Quraysh (The Battle of The Combined Forces).

convention when deemed the best option and on war and force when peace and convention could not be invoked.

He started [the event of Al-Hudaybiyah] by calling for Hajj, and did not confine his invitation to Muslims believing in his mission, but he extended it to all Arab clans that join Muslims in gratifying the House [Kaaba in Mecca] and travel to. And in so doing, he engaged himself and all Arabs in one same cause against Quraysh, and in one same interest against Quraysh's interest. This way, he separated clearly between Quraysh and all other Arabs in the call and cause, and spoiled Quraysh's cunning in inciting the Arabic pride to engage against Muhammad and his Islamic call. For Muhammad and his companions were not heedless about the Arab pride such that they humiliate or suppress its glory. [With this], Muslims associated themselves with Arabs, so that the Arabs will triumph rather than degrade when these Muslims triumph. And Muslims allied with the Arabs so that they do not cut off what is between them and their fathers and forefathers. And when they conflict with Quraysh, they do so with Quraysh only and their associates, but not with all other Arab clans.

Through his political skills, Prophet Muhammad (PBUH) refuted what Quraysh deliberately claimed to anger Arabs at Islam in that it cuts off businesses and threatens those markets visited by the pilgrimages and benefit people travelling to and from Mecca. For here he is! Muhammad himself in the company of his followers and others are on their way to perform pilgrimage, and interrupting this journey is an act of crime that brings wrath on the perpetrator and those behind it. And in such case, no one can blame Muslims for issues of business and market interruptions.

We have heard in the modern times about the passive resistance or the resistance that avoid violence and rely on nothing other than rightfulness and reasoning. We knew about this in India by Gandhi and was pursued by his followers, which caused much nuisance to the British government more than what bombs and bloody riots would have done. It was said then that Gandhi learned this from the Great Russian reformer Leon Tolstoy. And it was also said that it is more likely that Gandhi learned this from the Hindu and Buddhist cultures that had banned harm to animals, let alone humans, before Tolstoy established his new principle.

And those who adopted the last opinion ruled out the possibility that Muslims, Buddhists, and Hindus could have agreed to Gandhi's movement and his proclamation of this passive resistance. And in discarding Islam's consent to passive resistance, they postulated that, since Islam has legislated fighting, it cannot be in agreement with what suits Buddhists and Hindus in terms of commitment to peace and avoidance of confrontation. But the example given by the Prophet (PBUH) in the way he handled the complexity of the event of Al-Hudaybiyah refutes this argument and shows clearly that Islam has drawn from each what assists in proclaiming the call at a time and measure that suits every situation and condition. In fact, the Prophet (PBUH) relied neither on war alone nor on peace alone; rather he borrowed from them both what suited and used both combined when suited, and he was the one who judged as he saw fit, rather than being lifelessly leaning on one side toward either peace or war coercively.

The Prophet was going to Mecca for pilgrimage not invasion, and he was saying this and repeating it, with evidences manifest to whoever asks. He provided evidences to his intention by being disarmed, except with what would normally be allowed to be carried by nonfighters.

And in doing so, not only did he separate Quraysh from all Arabs, but he also separated Quraysh from the Abyssinians and made the chiefs and wise people disagree in their reactions to his move as to whether he should be accepted or engaged in a truce. And in doing so, he was stressing to his companions that they must exercise peace and patience in an effort to prevent his rivals from uniting under one opinion. And only a few of his companions understood his aim, including the elites.

When the two parties [Muslims and Quraysh] eventually agreed to a truce of peace, the policy of the Prophet in accepting the harsh conditions imposed by Quraysh reflects absolute wisdom and diplomacy, the term used by modern politicians.

[In that treaty], he asked Ali Ibn Abi Taleb to write: "In the Name of Allah, The Most Gracious, The Most Merciful;" Suhayl Ibn Amro, the delegate from Quraysh, objected, saying: "I do not know him as Al-Rahman [the Most Gracious], Al-Rahim [the Most Merciful]. Write only: Bismika Allahumma [in Your Name, Oh Allah]." The Prophet (PBUH) agreed and dictated: "This is a treaty between Muhammad the Messenger of Allah and Suhayl Ibn Amro." "Stop!" Cried Suhayl. "If I thought you were Allah's Messenger, I would not be fighting against you, would I? Write your name and your father's." And it is narrated that Ali hesitated [to erase it] and the Prophet erased it by his own hand and dictated that he writes: "Muhammad Ibn Abdullah," instead.

They then agreed that Muslims must send back any Meccan who did not have their guardian's permission to embrace Islam; and agreed that Muslims wishing to leave Islam are permitted to return to Mecca, and that the Arab clans are permitted to join either Muhammad or Quraysh in the treaty.

They also agreed that Muslims should go back to Madinah immediately but that they could return the following year for the pilgrimage with no weapons, except what nonfighters usually carry [swords in their bags] and that they would stay in Mecca for three days.

Had the articles of this treaty been written after Muslims had triumphed in a war, it would have been written differently, and the polytheists would have accepted his prophethood either voluntarily or forcibly and would not have been entitled to get back anyone from their servants or minors who accept Islam and join Muslims. But the treaty was a peace truce or a treaty to stop hostility actions for a period of time, as called nowadays. And in this context, there was no need to abide by certain protocols such as enforcing the titles of the representatives; nor was there a need to compel any of the two parties to compromise their own principles or ideologies. And had Muhammad insisted that Quraysh must return those who leave Islam, he would have then breached claim of both Islamic guidance and values. For the Muslim who leaves this Prophet voluntarily to join Quraysh is not really a Muslim and he would better join Quraysh rather than joining the Prophet of Islam.

But as for the Muslim who embraces Islam but returns to Quraysh in dignity [according to the unjust condition imposed by Quraysh], it is Islam that links him to the Prophet, and this is something that cannot be controlled by the polytheists and the relating connection does not depend on the distance. For no goodness is anticipated from the weak Muslim who leaves his Islam when tested and trialed. On the other hand, Muslims will incur no losses from the strong Muslim who holds on to his Islam.

It was soon after the treaty when Quraysh realized that the condition they presumed a winner for their side and a defeat for Muhammad (PBUH) is rather causing them havoc. For those

Muslims who rejected Quraysh but were not accepted by Muhammad, in his respect for the treaty, camped in an outside territory targeting Quraysh's business convoys, which were supposed to be safe during the period of the treaty. Quraysh was not able to complain to the Prophet, since these folks were outside his jurisdiction according to the treaty; neither was Quraysh able to keep them in Mecca as they presumed when they imposed this condition while writing the articles of the treaty. And had the Prophet accepted authority over those who fled from Quraysh, it would have been possible that Quraysh might had knocked the treaty or asked the Prophet to respect the condition.

The treaty was indeed accomplished! And those who did not know soon realized how much Islam benefited from it. For those who wished to, but could not ally with the Prophet [before the treaty] were then able to do so publicly. And the Prophet put to rest his struggle with Quraysh and applied himself to the Jews of Khaiber and foreign states and sent delegates inviting them to Islam. And he also opened the doors to delegates that denounced Quraysh's injustice and can now support Islam openly without subjecting themselves to the irresistible brunt of confrontation with Quraysh.

And when the noble verse was revealed right after the treaty: "*Verily, We have granted you a manifest victory – Quran, 48:1*," majority of the companions did not understand what it meant and could not see where the victory is in this treaty, which they instead deemed a mere surrender. But they understood what type of victory the treaty was after two years, and they realized that some victory could be achieved without weaponry, in what may appear as a defeat in the eyes of the hasty who lacks long sightedness.

THE MANIFEST VICTORY

In that year, there was a victory that could only be perceived by the one who could see tomorrow's events, but not by the one who could just see the present. However, it had been only one year before this victory was seen by those who could see except with their physical eyes. And with this victory, some were pleased and some were upset.

In the year following the treaty, the Prophet called upon his companions to prepare for Hajj, with none of those who witnessed the treaty of Al-Hudaybiyah to be left behind. They then all marched desirously after the previous ban like a patient after relief, except those who were martyred in Khaiber or died in that year. And with them marched a big crowd of those who did not witness Al-Hudaybiyah accompanied by women and children. They drove with them sixty camels ready for sacrifice. They also carried weapons, shields, and arrows in a hundred knights lead by Muhammad Ibn Maslama.

When the Prophet and his companions arrived at Zi Al-Holaifa[24], he put the horses forward. Quraysh heard the news, got concerned and sent Mekrez Ibn Hafs and others to meet Prophet Muhammad (PBUH). They said: "Oh Muhammad, you have never been known in your youth or adulthood as being treacherous. You marched to your people with weaponry despite the condition that you must carry only the arm that nonfighters are allowed: swords in their bags." The Prophet said: "I am not carrying this weaponry through," and Mekrez said: "This is what we know about you: faithfulness and dutifulness."

In fact, the Prophet carried the weaponry as a precautionary measure, as he said to his companions: "If someone attacks us from Quraysh, we would be relatively close to our weapons." And he left the weapons guarded in a place accessible to him near Mecca. The Prophet then marched on his camel (Al-Qaswaa) with the Muslim crowd around him holding their swords and chanting. Abdullah Ibn Rawaha[25] was holding the rope of the camel and chanting:

"Oh disbelievers, stay away from his way, as the goodness is with the Prophet."

"Oh God, I believe in his say, as I saw the truth in accepting it."

And in his zeal, Ibn Rawaha was almost on the brink of crying for war against Quraysh. But Umar stopped him, and the Prophet

---

[24] Translator: A place
[25] Translator: A poet and companion of the Prophet

advised him to just say: "There is no God but Allah, has made truth [fulfilled] His promise and aided His servant and defeated the enemy armies Alone." Ibn Rawaha chanted this with his loud voice and Muslims followed him with the echo resonating from the sides of the valley so that those who left Mecca at night and wished to avoid the convoy of the Prophet could still hear it.

The pilgrimage was then a triumph sighted by those whose insights could not perceive it on the day of Al-Hudaybiyah. And with it, many people embraced Islam after rejection, including the weak and strong ones: some of them were impressed by the Prophet fulfilling his promises although he had the power to breach it; some were taken by the attributes of Islam and the mutual compassion among Muslims plus the aspect of their obedience and dedication to the Prophet; and some realized that Islam will eventually prevail, so they opted for peace. In this regard, it suffices that the outcomes of the treaty of Al-Hudaybiyah persuaded Khalid Ibn Al-Waleed and Amro Ibn Al-Aas[26] of Muhammad's prophethood; and those two, despite their differences, were equal in terms of outstanding intelligence and excellent disposition, albeit in different ways.

And thus the genius of Muhammad had manifested in managing political affairs, as it had manifested in leading armies. And his tactics brought outstanding success when he called for pilgrimage without conquering Mecca in numbers or weaponry;

[26] Translator: Two great companions of the Prophet.

it was success when he called upon Muslims and non-Muslims to join him in his journey; it was success when he opted to embrace peace and establish proofs while marching to his aim; it was success when he accepted the articles of the treaty that proved difficult to be accepted even by his closest circle; and it was success when he was able to see beyond the day and later achieved his goals.

CHAPTER 5: MUHAMMAD'S MANAGERIAL GENIUS

PERSONAL ABILITIES

ISLAM IS FULL OF RULES that can fall within the scope of humans' management skills, as we call them today. For example, Islam is full of recommendations about dealings such as renting, sales, loans, pre-emptive rights, commerce plus other living and social affairs that are quoted by legislators at all times.

Yet while writing about the Prophet, we do not aim to recite the Islamic jurisprudence or elaborate on the religion instructions, as these are available elsewhere. But instead, we want to present the Prophet's deeds and injunctions from the angle of his personal abilities and psychological characteristics that accompanied him while delivering his religious message or undertaking other non-religious human matters.

Also, we are not interested in addressing the management side as those written instructions and protocols used to manage offices with all associated details, since these fall within the scope of subordinate executives rather than those who command. What is addressed here are the intellectual, managerial abilities that enable someone to create a well-founded management structure and then leave the details to others to pursue.

For it is not possible for someone who is naturally disorderly and irresponsible to establish a successful management system, even if he is otherwise intelligent and determined, whereas the character that has natural propensity to devise successful managerial system is the one who is both disciplined and responsible and embraces the principle of specialization rather than assigning the same task to many individuals, leading to inconsistent results. And this trait existed in Muhammad (PBUH) in its best form; he used to apply the concept of leadership whenever he faced a social or society situation that required any concerting effort.

And among his cited sayings: "If three people go on a journey, they should appoint one of them to lead." And in his management, he used to name the leader, the deputy leader, and the deputy of the deputy leader when he commissions the army, in case there is a sequence of casualty. And in this, he had two crucial conditions for leadership and commandment: competency and liking. He said: "If a man leads ten people while knowing that there is a more competent person within the band, he has then cheated Allah, his Messenger, and Muslims." And he also said: "Whoever leads people in prayers while they hate him, his prayers will not go beyond his ear [i.e. will not be accepted]."

And he was keen to ensure that responsibilities, big or small, are entrusted in those who are capable of undertaking them, in accordance with the premise he laid: "Every one of you is a shepherd and is responsible for his flock. The leader of people is a guardian and is responsible for his subjects. A man is the guardian of his family and he is responsible for them. A woman is the guardian of her husband's home and his children and she is responsible for them. The servant of a man is a guardian of the property of his master and he is responsible for it. Surely, every one of you is a shepherd and responsible for his flock."

What Islam forbade or permitted was known to majority of Muslims, whether from Al-Ansaar [The Helpers from Madinah] or Mohajerin [Emigrants from Mecca to Madinah]. Yet he (PBUH) did not let anyone claim the right to apply Islamic laws or to force people to obey a command or to stop a breach, except for those in an authority position who are entitled to manage peoples' affairs. For example, when some of the Muslims killed a man during the conquest of Mecca, the Prophet got upset, and he said clearly: "...so if anyone tells you that the Prophet fought in Mecca, say that Allah permitted him to do this but did not permit you the clan of Khuza'ah." The other example was when he wanted to confiscate wines, he followed an approach to be learned and adopted. Ibn Umar narrated: "The Prophet asked me to bring a knife and sent it to be sharpened. He then gave it to me and said: "Bring it over to me tomorrow," and I did. He marched with his companions to the wine lane in Madinah market, which had wine bags from Shaam[27]. He took the knife and tore these bags and gave it back to me. He then asked the companions he brought with to join me and help. He

[27] Translator: Region now including Syria, Lebanon, Jordan, Palestine and parts of Turkey

commanded me to drop by all markets and tear every wine bag I come across, and I did, without sparing any bag." This is an act of a manager and an act of the Prophet who explained what is Halal [lawful] and what is Haram [unlawful].

Drinking, selling or transportation of wine are unlawful acts known to every Muslim, whether that Muslim studied or did not study the religion. But those socially forbidden acts must be controlled by the person in charge, rather than being left in the hand of anyone who knows what is lawful and what is unlawful, for the matter here is not in the legality but in managing and execution [of the Islamic law] in a lively society that accommodates arrays of interests and desires. And such society would not be plagued by something worse than chaos and disorder, conflict of claims as well as disobedience and oblivion to those in power. So the Prophet was not just content with the explicit judgement in that Quran has made wine unlawful, neither was he content with assigning someone of no capacity to apply the law, but he took to the street by himself and commanded someone in particular and certain individuals to continue the work he started. And he did not allow anyone else to apply the law as he wishes.

We have heard recently much about security and order as well as upholding laws and legislations. Yet we have not heard in this regard something more comprehensive and sound than what the Prophet said: "Compliance and obedience are rights, except in sins, which warrant no compliance or obedience." He also said in the narration by Obada Ibn Al-Samet: "We do not dispute one's authority unless we see from him manifest blasphemy with evidence from Allah." And he said: "A wrongful ruler is better than riot, and both are evil", and said: "A suspicious ruler can ruin people", plus other sayings on the subject that are comprehensive in the course of wise management and straightforward, sound principles between the ruler and his people.

So it is an order overlain by power, and that power is overlain by a manifest evidence from the law and mind, and all of these are associated with tolerance that does not pursue disputes and push suspicions or exaggerate toward extremism.

This sound, powerful revelation of managing the interest of the nation and handling the affairs of societies was what inspired the Prophet to advise on health issues and prevention of epidemics in a clear saying well before germs were discovered and before quarantines were established among nations some tens of centuries before our modern time: "If you hear that the plaque exists in a place, do not approach it, and if it occurs in your place, do not leave it." This is an advice of someone who, in his acts, cares about the complete human world not the interest of one single city or one single individual. For there is nothing better protective to the world than confining an epidemic into a location, and it is not the right of a specific town to seek its own safety or the safety of one of its citizens by exposing all other towns to that epidemic.

MANAGEMENT OF GENERAL AFFAIRS

However, the excellent management manifests in tackling general affairs that incite looming conflicts and disorder. For management is different from all these cast articles and rules that can be applied by the ruler like machines and robots that have only one way to function. Rather, it is in most cases handling souls and managing risks with no warranty against little deviation here and there.

And this is where Muhammad's genius was perfect in bringing about success and avoiding troubles. For he never faced a difficult situation before or after his prophethood but handled it with the best of opinions and the closest resolution to peace and satisfaction. He did this [before Islam] when each clan [in Quraysh] claimed the right to relocate the Blackstone [of Kaaba][28], which is an honor not to be waived; and seizure of this honor by any single clan would have invoked dire consequences, even if this seizure was a result of coincidence or a mere draw. Muhammad then provided the best advice that could not be overruled by something wiser at the time or in the future. He brought a blanket and placed the Blackstone in the middle and asked every chief of a clan to hold to one end of the blanket and

[28] Translator: This is a small, sacred piece of rock in Kaaba

lift it. It was his resolution after this to hold the Blackstone and place it by his own hands to where it belonged undisputedly by any of the rivals. And in doing this, it was as if he was borrowing from tomorrow the call that was hidden in the future. And had they [Quraysh] realized it [the future call for Islam], they would have not enjoyed any peace in his resolution [to solve the Blackstone crisis] and he would have rather been resented with hostility and hatred.

He also did something similar [after Islam] the day he arrived to Madinah migrating from Mecca when the various delegates competed to host him and provide dwelling, while he is concerned and keen not to instill jealousy by preferring some over the others or preferring a place over another. Accordingly, he left it up to his she-camel and let off its halter so that she can walk and stop freely while people were giving her space until she kneeled down voluntarily. And in doing this, the she-camel resolved potential future risk had any human otherwise decided on the issue, even with voidance of poor intention and ill thoughts.

And he did it again when he allotted the booty preferentially to those people from Mecca whose faith was weak, but did not provide for the Helpers [Al-Ansaar] who had strong faith and persevered in their struggle for Islam. So when those Helpers got furious at the way the booty was distributed, no one was faster than the Prophet in addressing the issue and pleasing them with irrefutable logic in a way that showed them that they have the best share, the best justification and the best persuasion, simultaneously: "You Helpers, do you feel anxious for the [trivial] things of this world, wherewith I have sought to incline these people unto the faith in which you are already established? Are you not satisfied Oh group of Helpers that the people go with ewes and camels while you go along with the Messenger of Allah (PBUH) to your dwellings? By Him in Whose Hand is my life, had there been no emigration, I would have been one of the Helpers. Allah! Have mercy on the Helpers, their children, and their children's children."

These are words of someone whose management and leadership are natural traits in his disposition and formation. For he is the manager when management is to run affairs, and he is the manager when management is emotional intelligence. He is competent and confident in tackling tasks associated with potential disorders and faults because he applies discipline and accountability, specialty, and tolerance. And with this traits, you will not find in a society a hole for imbalance, dissolution or cracks in managing affairs.

CHAPTER 6: THE MESSAGE DELIVERER

"BY ALLAH, HAVE I DELIVERED THE MESSAGE?" This is the standing phrase that the Prophet kept repeating in his last and longest speech, the farewell speech.

And this standing phrase has great meaning in its context, because it summarized a full life in a few words. For the life of the Prophet was not but a life of announcements and message delivery, in his acts, sayings, mobility, and stillness. And the best conclusion to his life (PBUH) is what he said at the time of death: "The glory of my exalted Lord, for I have delivered!"

And for the truth implied in the meaning of the standing phrase, you realize that the overwhelming feature of the narrations reserved from the Prophet's sayings is indeed 'message delivery'. It is actually more than this, for it is the most comprehensive that dwarfs all other features, since it is the inclusive root to all other peripheral ones that derived from it. The words the prophets said are documented: treaties or letters he sent, talks, supplications, recommendations, and answers that were written after him and subjected to effortful scrutiny regarding consistency and authenticity.

Delivery is the common feature of the art that includes all of the legacy above, even things that were narrated in the form of stories, orders to subordinates or the prayers that the Prophet taught Muslims to supplicate to Allah. For example, examine the story of the three persons of the cave and their supplication with their good deeds as quoted in the selection made by the Scholar Muslem. As narrated from the Prophet: “While three people were setting out on a journey, they were overtaken by rain, and they had to find protection in a mountain cave where at its mouth there fell a rock of that mountain and thus blocked them altogether. One of them said to the others: “Look to your good deeds that you performed for the sake of Allah and then supplicate Allah, the Exalted, that He might rescue you [from this trouble].” One of them said: “Oh Allah, I had my parents who were old and my wife and my small children also. I tended the flock, and when I came back to them in the evening, I milked them [the sheep, goats, cows, etc.] and first served that milk to my parents. One day I was obliged to go out to a distant place in search of fodder, and I could not come back before evening and found them [the parents] asleep. I milked the animals as I used to milk and brought milk to them and stood by their heads avoiding to disturb them from sleep and I did not deem it advisable to serve milk to my children before serving them. My children wept near my feet. I remained there in that very state and my parents too until it was morning. And (Oh Allah) if you are aware that I did this in order to seek your pleasure, grant us riddance from this trouble.” The rock slipped a bit that they could see the sky. The second one said: “Oh Allah, I had a female cousin whom I loved more than the men love the women. I wanted to have sexual intercourse with her; she refused but on the condition of getting one hundred dinars [for necessity]. It was with very great difficulty that I could collect one hundred dinars and then paid them to her and when I was going to have sexual intercourse with her, she said: “Servant of Allah, fear Allah and do not break the seal [of chastity] but by lawful means.” I got up. Oh Allah, if you are aware that I did this in order to seek your pleasure, rid us from this trouble.” The situation was somewhat eased for them. The third one said: “Allah, I employed a workman for a measure of rice. After he had finished his work I gave him his dues [in the form of] a measure of rice, but he did not accept them. I used these rice as seeds, and that gave a bumper crop, and I became wealthy enough to have cows and flocks [in my possession]. He came to me and said: “Fear Allah, and commit no cruelty upon me in regard to my dues.” I said to him: “Takeaway this flock of cows and sheep.” He said: “Fear Allah and do not make a fun of me.” I said: “I am not making a fun of you. You take the cows and the flocks.” So he took them. “Oh Allah, if you are aware that I did it for your pleasure, ease the situation for us.” And Allah relieved them from the rest of the trouble.”

DIRECTING EMIRS AND COMMANDERS

This was his way (PBUH) of teaching by storytelling. Look at his way in directing emirs and commanders as narrated by Scholar Muslem. “The Prophet used to advise his commander over an army or a platoon, to first fear Allah and be dutiful to his Muslim fellows before adding: “Conquer in the name of Allah and in the cause of Allah, fight the disbelievers, conquer but do not overkill, do not betray, do not disfigure, and do not kill a child. And when you confront your disbelieving enemies, invite them to accept one of three, and approve them for what they choose: call them to join the emigrants [i.e. become Muslims], and advise them that if they do they would be entitled to the same rights; and if they refuse, invite them to be like the Muslim Bedouins but with no entitlement to booty or spoils until they fight with Muslims; and if they still refuse, ask them to pay the levy, and approve them if they accept. But if they refuse, ask Allah’s help and fight them. And if you besiege people in a fortress and they ask you for a covenant for protection, do not provide them with the covenant of Allah and His Messenger, but give them the covenant under your name and your companions. For breaching your own covenant would be of less gravity than breaching the covenant of Allah and the covenant of his Messenger.”

“And if you besiege people in a shelter and ask you to surrender, provided you apply the verdict of Allah, do not accept that you implement the verdict of Allah, but accept that you apply your own verdict, for you do not know whether you really hit the verdict of Allah.” And thus was his way of teaching his commanders orders and recommendations.

Now look at his letters style as seen from his example to Negus[29]: "Salutations, I entertain Allah's praise, there is no God but He, the Sovereign, the Holy, the Source of peace, the Giver of peace, the Guardian of faith, the Preserver of safety. I bear witness that Jesus, the son of Mary, is the Spirit of Allah and His Word, which He cast into Mary, the virgin, the good, the pure so that she conceived Jesus. Allah created him from His spirit and His breathing as He created Adam by His Hand. I call you to Allah alone with no associate and to His obedience and to follow me and to believe in that which came to me, for I am the Messenger of Allah. I sent you my cousin Gaafar and a band of Muslims; when they come to you, accommodate them and avoid tyranny. For I invite you and your men to Allah; I hereby bear witness that I have communicated my message and advice. Peace be upon him who follows true guidance."

TREATIES AND COVENANTS

And here is an example of his style in treaties and covenants as appeared in his document (PBUH) in the pact between the Emigrants and Helpers (Al-Ansaar) on the one hand and the Jews on the other hand.

"The Emigrants of Quraysh unite together and shall pay blood money among themselves, and shall ransom honorably their prisoners."

---

[29] Translator: The king of Ethiopia at the time

"Every tribe of the Helpers unite together, as they were at first, and every section among them will pay a ransom for acquitting its relative prisoners," etc.

These are typical examples of the wording of the Prophet (PBUH) in topics that they differ in their nature the same way the stories, commands, letters and pacts differ, but they all have the same unique feature, that is 'message delivery' or 'clear communication.' And the most accurate way to describe it is to refer to its analogy with the definition of the 'straight line,' quoted in geometry as being the shortest path connecting two points. For there is no way shorter than this style in delivering a message.

The characteristics that are more suitable to observe in the Prophet's wording as examples and models for Arabic rhetoric are the absence of sophistication, obscurity, and eccentricity plus absence or rarity of strange words. For there was nothing difficult for a listener to understand nor was there anything that required repetition or elaboration in the words of Muhammad, who was from Quraysh [i.e. the heart of Arabs], brought up in Banu Saad [the most fluent Arab clan], and knowledgeable on the dialects of the various Arab tribes. And the reason for this [clarity of Muhammad's wording style] is that his concern was to convey the message without putting a barrier of strange words or meaning between him and his listener(s). This is why it was narrated that he used to repeat the word three times to ensure comprehension, and he used to dislike over-wording or priding on rhetoric, saying: "Verily, Allah dislikes the eloquent person who rolls his tongue [in exaggeration] as a cow rolls its tongue [while eating]."

And in his public and private life, the Prophet was taciturn and avoidant of chitchat; he used to utter only the truth, even in his jokes. It is not unexpected then that his speech was free from waffle, repetition, and excessiveness. However, when he repeated some words in some of his treaties, it was the act that suited treaties, where repetition of a word implies invariability of its intended meaning, which is a feature of message delivery needed in treaties and indicates emphasis and affirmation. While on other occasions, he repeated words deliberately for more comprehension.

In the Prophet's letter to Negus, there was more mention of Allah's beautiful names and reference to Jesus and his mother compared to his other letters, but these were mandatory in the context of addressing a Christian king who needed to know how Allah and Jesus were similarly described in his religion and in Islam, the religion he is being invited to, and he [Negus] could still see the differences if he desires. This is the delivery style in the way the Prophet expressed himself: every word reaches the listener, and every word is meant with a predetermined measure.

And in doing the above, there are no decoration, tricks or difficulty of someone who exaggerates the impact, but rather a delivery that suits manhood and dignity; and the other party must bear the consequences of rejecting the delivered message after this clarity.

RHYME LIKE BEAUTIFUL ORNAMENT

The Prophet disliked the rhymes used by religious ministers in their tricks to deceive their audience into thinking that what they are hearing is the talisman of magicians and devils. However, he did not reject the rhyme entirely, and he did not abstain from the rhyme that flows naturally. And in most cases, this was in what was recited publicly like the Azaan [call for prayers] or in his comprehensive recommendations, as in his saying: "What is the matter with people who stipulate conditions that are not in the Book of Allah? Whoever stipulates something that is not in the Book of Allah, it is not valid even if he stipulates one hundred conditions! The condition of Allah is more deserving of being followed and is more hinting," and his saying[30]: "Allah has made it prohibited for you to be disrespectful (showing undutiful behavior) to your mothers, to bury your daughters alive, to refuse others (their dues), and to demand things from others (which are not worth demanding), and He hates that you engage in gossip, asking many questions about people's affairs and wasting wealth."

---

[30] Translator: The rhymes cited here are in the Arabic language and may not be appreciated in the English translation provided here.

And his way in this beautiful quality is typical of his ways in all of his other beautiful qualities a man is entitled to: strength in his wording and strength in his rhythm. For his rhyme (PBUH) was like the gold ornament that fits a man, no more.

Abu Sufyan [a leader in Quraysh] wrote him a letter ended with: "...we want from you half of Madinah's yield of date; answer, otherwise I warn you of destruction of your homes and uproot of your traces:

[POEM] The clans answered from Nezar [an Arab tribe] to give victory to Al-Latt [One of Quraysh's biggest Idols] in the Sacred House [Kaaba], and the lions from Quraysh marched on marked horses inciting fire."

"نريد منك نصف نخل المدينة، فإن أجبتنا إلى ذلك، وإلا أبشر بخراب الديار وقلع الآثار.

تجـاوبت القبــائل مـن نـزار لنصـر اللات في البيت الحرام

وأقبلت الضراغم من قريش على خيـل مسـومــة ضــرام."

The Prophet replied with a letter saying: "The book of the people of polytheism and hypocrisy, blasphemy and dispute has arrived, and I understood your message. By Allah, my answer to you is the tips of the arrows and the blades of the swords. So stop worshipping the idols, otherwise expect bangs with the swords, fracture of your heads and destruction of your homes and uproot of your traces."

"وصل كتاب أهل الشرك والنفاق والكفر والشقاق، وفهمت مقالتهم، فوالله مالكم عندي جواب إلاّ أطراف الرماح، وأشغار الصفح، فارجعوا ويلكم من عبادة الأصنام، وأبشروا بضرب الحسام وبفلق الهام، وخراب الديار وقلع الآثار."

The rhyme of the Prophet in this situation is the best style that suits communication with people of the time of ignorance [i.e. before Islam], as it reflects confidence, power, bravery, and threat. And this is why the Prophet [after Islam] accepted the wording of the pact between his grandfather and the clan of Khuza'ah [that was formulated before Islam] despite the rhyme and grandiloquence used for confirmation and emphasis of sacred rites. And here is the text:

"In the name of Allah; this is the pact between Abdulmotalib Ibn Hashem to Khuza'ah, a pact that unites but does not disunite: elders to elders, youngsters to youngsters, and the present to the absent. They agreed and contracted firmly adopting the most affirmed pact that cannot be breached or broken as long as the sun rises over the Mountain Thabir, a camel walks by a desert, the two mountains in Mecca remain and a person inhabits Mecca; a contract that must last forever, supported by a hot rising sun and a countless number of dark nights. Abdulmatalib with his children and followers from the Arabs and the men of Khuza'ah are shoulders to shoulders in cooperation and support. It is incumbent on Abdulmotalib to aid Khuza'ah with his people, and it is incumbent on Khuza'ah to aid Abdulmotalib and his sons and followers against all Arabs in the east or west, difficult or flat territories. The two parties make Allah their surety and his bearing is sufficient."

"باسمك اللهم، هذا ما تحالف عليه عبد المطلب بن هاشم لخزاعة حلفاً جامعاً غير مفرق، الأشياخ على الأشياخ، والأصاغر على الأصاغر، والشاهد على الغائب. وتعاهدوا وتعاقدوا أوكد عهد وأوثق عقد، لا ينقض ولا ينكث، ما أشرقت شمس على ثبير وحن بفلاة بعير، وما قام الأخشبان، وعمر بمكة إنسان، حلف أبد لطول أمد، يزيده طلوع الشمس شداً، وظلام الليل سداً. وإن عبد المطلب وولده ومن معهم دون سائر بني النضر بن كنانة، ورجال خزاعة، متكافئون متضافرون متعاونون. فعلى عبد المطلب النصرة لهم ممن تابعه على كل طالب وتر، في بر أو بحر أو سهل أو وعر. وعلى خزاعة النصرة لعبد المطلب وولده ومن معهم على جميع العرب، في شرق أو غرب، أو حزن أو سهب. وجعلوا الله على ذلك كفيلا، وكفى به حميلاً."

These are examples of the rhyme that the Prophet uttered or approved. The decoration [in wording] that accompanied these cases was for delivering the required message without exaggeration. And the thing that helped the Prophet in adopting the style of message delivery is that people around him were listening to a beloved and obeyed Prophet. For he was naturally accessible to their souls with no tricks; he was attractive to their hearing without a need for suspense, and he was embracive of such moderation that did not need excessiveness, but simultaneously did not suffer flaws.

And as for his messages to kings and emirs who did not embrace Islam, these were for delivering the message in its essence, leaving the elaboration and explanation to those [Muslim delegates or representatives] who are entrusted to provide guidance and answer queries. As such, his style in these messages was to ensure that the delivery is efficient and that it is free from both excessiveness and shortcomings.

And we say that the two elements [strength in the saying and decoration of the words] helped the Prophet in his style of message delivery, although we cannot say that they forced it or inspired it. For the little narrations preserved from the early days of the Islamic call before propagation of the religion had the same style of the Prophet, that is freedom from overacting and excessiveness. The real source of the strength of the Prophet's style of message delivery was his confidence in what he says rather than his confidence in those who listen to him. As such, his style was consistent in this regard: a style of simplicity and dignity, and his context was natural with no twisting. And this was reflected in his recommendations to his followers to shorten sermons and speak less, the same advice he provided to his workers.

However, it should not be understood that the context or situation did not impact the wording style of the Prophet. For he (PBUH) used to observe the difference [in the context] and accommodate it. For example, he used to lean on a bow when giving a war speech and lean on a stick upon delivering a sermon. Also, his face was used to reflect his emotions when he experienced anger or delivered a warning: "When he (PBUH) delivered sermons, his eyes became red, his voice rose, and his anger increased so that he was like one giving a warning against the enemy and saying: "The enemy has made a morning attack on you and in the evening too.""

MODERN STYLE

For some, the style of the Prophet – in his sayings and letters – is a contemporary style that can be used as an example for people in our time and beyond. For the style that comes from a straight soul is a modern style for all eras. And it is a mistake if someone assumes that connecting sentences was a condition in the old Arabic style, whereas separating sentences is a condition for modern Arabic styles. And it is also a mistake if someone assumes that accommodation of punctuation marks is an indication of any of these two types of style. Take for example, the prophetic saying quoted above: "What is the matter with people who stipulate conditions that are not in the Book of Allah? Whoever stipulates something that is not in the Book of Allah, it is not valid even if he stipulates one hundred conditions? The condition of Allah is more deserving of being followed and is more hinting." This saying accommodated the Arabic rhetoric in the way it connected or separated between sentences, but it also accommodated the modern style in its punctuation marks, and is therefore an evidence of the error made by those who differentiate the Arabic rhetoric on that basis.

OPINION OF THE PROPHET ON POEM

We have received only a few of the comments of the Prophet on poem and poets that are not a technical critique, but they measured the words [of others] against goodness, reforms, and compliance with the rules of the religion, the habits of truth and fidelity. An example is his saying (PBUH): "The most truthful word is the one said by Poet Lobaid: "Indeed everything other than Allah is false,"" and his saying about Poet Amro'a Al-Qays that he will be the holder of the fire flag of poets in hell. He used to quote some poem but changing [unintentionally] the measure while maintaining the meaning. So he was heard saying: "And will deliver to you the news that person who you have not paid," which is short enough to maintain the meaning. But when he repeated the saying of Sohaim Abd Ibn Al-Hashaas: "Hoariness and Islam are sufficient for someone to refrain [behave]," he swapped the words 'Hoariness' and 'Islam,' saying: "Islam and hoariness are sufficient for someone to refrain." In doing this, he refuted any claim of himself being a poet and that Quran is a series of recited poems as alleged by the disbelievers, [since this ruined the measure by this rearrangement of the words].

And he (PBUH) hailed poems that praise and defend Islam and Muslims. And his attitude in this regard was similar to those expressed by prophets accepting good words. For they were sent to teach people goodness and righteousness rather than basics of critique and composition.

CONCISENESS OF SPEECH

Yet the strongest feature in the Prophet's ability to deliver messages is the power to include the best values in the most concise way; it is even the power to sum complete knowledge in a few words, which may otherwise warrant volumes of books to explain.

One example relates to the behavioral knowledge in life and religion, which the Prophet summarized in less than two short lines: "Work for your life as if you live forever, and work for your hereafter as if you will die tomorrow."

Another example relates to politics knowledge, which he summed up in his saying: "Your rulers shall be of your very own caliber." What pillars and rules that may govern a nation's affairs that are not included in this statement! The saying implies that people are responsible for their government, and people will be accountable for the actions of a government, regardless of any ignorance or compulsion [in installing such government]; for any ignorance eventually belongs to the people and any compulsion derives from the weaknesses they are punished for [by having the wrong government]. And it implies that what really matters is the manners of the nation before the systems or structures of a government. For there is no room for injustice in a nation that hates injustice, even if ruled by someone who does not embrace justice. Similarly, there is no room for a nation to breath liberty if it does not comprehend the notion of liberty, even if ruled by someone who is bound by a thousand constraints of laws and forms [about liberty and freedom].

And it implies that the government is an effect rather than a cause, for Allah does not change what is in a nation unless they change what is in themselves [rephrased Quranic saying, 13:11].

It also implies that the power is vested in people. And it means that a nation deserves the governing system that it strives and perseveres for, even if this government is not the one that vouch for reforms and independence.

And thus is the message delivery [of the Prophet] that fruits invariably in all courses and directions!

Another example in his knowledge (PBUH) on responsibilities is his saying: "The people who suffer the worst hardships are the prophets, then those next in rank, then those after them, and so forth." For human talents and advantages bring duties and burdens rather than enjoyment and extravagance. Man's knowledge of good and evil brings about the trialing responsibilities and does not spare him to the rest and relaxation he may seek, for this knowledge is a liability the same way intelligence is a liability.

There are countless numbers of similar examples in areas of politics, ethics, and sociology, for Muhammad (PBUH) was [broadly] eloquent in his words, in his tongue, and in his delivery. And he was fluent with the ability to deliver in the simplest style in terms of value and sufficiency, and he was by his tongue and heart among the Messengers and the model for the Messengers.

CHAPTER 7: MUHAMMAD, THE FRIEND

KIND AND WARMHEARTED

WHEN A PERSON LOVES PEOPLE and reversely deserves their love, he has then possessed the means of friendship from all angles. In this context, the means of friendship depend on the magnitude of the human emotions, decency, strong values, and loyalty trait, since a person may love people but may be lacking the decency, which drives them away and makes them distaste his love.

However, it is not sufficient for someone to be just a loving and decent person to reach the pinnacle of friendship, for he could be loving, beloved, and decent but with weak manners and loyalty that do not sustain a friendship or maintain a relationship. Friendship becomes complete with the adequacy of lively emotions, decency, and strong ethics; and Muhammad (PBUH) was the best example among the best of Allah's creation in this aspect. He was kind, merciful, life-long sociable to his acquaintances, despite the possible differences in age, race, and status.

He was a 12-year-old boy when his uncle was travelling and he clung to his uncle who eventually did not wish to leave him alone, so he took him aboard.

And he was (PBUH) an old man approaching his 60s when he wept unforgettably on the verge of his mother's grave. And there is no human record that matched the best, most generous, and kindest act of him toward his nurse Halima while he was in his 40s, saying: "My mother, my mother," where he would furnish his garment for her, as if he recalled her favor in feeding him as a baby. And he would give her camels and sheep that provide for her in a full drought year.

And in the aftermath of the Battle of Hunain, the defeated clan of Hawazin came to him and with them was his uncle from wet nursing. For this uncle of his, the Prophet interceded to Muslims that they must return the spoils, women, and children to the clan of Hawazin; and he even paid those who refused to return the spoils voluntarily.

In his childhood, he was under the care of a foreign female slave that he never stopped being dutiful to for the rest of his life, and he was concerned that she must be in a happy marriage the same way a father would be concerned for his daughters, saying to his companions: "Whoever wishes to marry to a woman from paradise let him marry Umm Ayman." And he continued calling her "Mum" every time he saw or talked to her. And in one of the battles, he saw her praying in her non-Arabic tongue, yet the battle did not distract him from listening to her and pay her a kind gesture.

This was his style of kindness to every weak person, even if not for a kind act he received from that person in his childhood. For he never shouted or beat a servant. Anas [the Prophet's servant] said: "I served the Prophet for 10 years: he never said to me 'ugh' once, and he never said why you did this for something I did, or why you did not do this for something I did not do." And he was the best smiley person and noblest in the soul with a pure heart; if he dislikes something, it is seen in his face, and when he likes something people around him take the heed.

His kindness accommodated all living things, not only people from his kith and kin and others. He used to lower the cup for the cat to drink; and he expressed sympathy with his servant's little brother over the death of the bird he was playing with. And he advised Muslims: "When you ride any of these animals, make sure you give them enough rest and do not treat them like devils." And he repeated: "Fear Allah in regards to these dumb animals; so ride them in goodness and eat them in goodness."

And he said: "Allah forgave a prostitute who saw a dog dying of thirst while approaching a water well; she took her shoes and tied it to her scarf and filled it with water for the dog to drink; Allah forgave her for that." And by the same token, he said: "A woman will be sent to the hellfire for a cat she tied; neither did she let her go to eat on her own nor did she feed her."

Furthermore, besides the living things, his kindness included non-living things, [and this was manifested in the way he used to name non-living things]. For example, he had a tray called the 'Coot', a sword called 'Zo Al-Faqqar', an armor coated in copper called 'Zat Al-Fodoul', a packsaddle called 'Al-Dag', a carpet called 'Al-Kaz, a pot called 'Al-Sader', a mirror called 'Almedallah', a scissors called Al-Game'a, and a bar called 'Al-Mamshouq'. And in naming these non-living things, there is a notion of affability that made them like living things that have characteristics and faces, as if each has its own distinctive personality that makes it special, the same way the beloved ones have distinctive faces, characters, and nicknames.

This human emotion that accommodated in its vastness everything around Prophet Muhammad (PBUH) was not the only means of friendship in this noble soul, but with it was a decency that is equally matching in sublimity and nobleness. And this decency was entrenched in the connection of the Prophet with people and in the way he regarded their feelings in the best way that utters generosity and bounty.

"And the Prophet was such that when one of his companions meets him and asks that he moves with him, he would move and does not leave until that companion leaves. And when one of his companions meets him and picks his hand, he would extend his hand and does not take it back until the companion does...." [Narration by one of the Prophet's companions].

"And he was such that when he says goodbye to someone and shakes hand, he would not take his hand back until the person does." [Narration by one of the Prophet's companions].

"And he was the most merciful to kids and families." "And when he comes back from a travel, he would greet the children of his family." [Narration by one of the Prophet's companions].

"And he was shyer than a virgin in her privacy, and the most patient over people's weaknesses." [Narration by one of the Prophet's companions].

He used to respect his companions both in their presence and absence. And he said: "Whoever looks into his brother's letter without permission, he looks into a piece of fire." [Narration by one of the Prophet's companions].

And with this human emotional intelligence, decency, and noble politeness, comes good looking, magnificent hygiene and keenness that people must see him in his best shape. In addition, he possessed honesty and trustworthiness that were conceded by his enemies, let alone his friends. In this context, it suffices to recall how people entrusted him with their valuables while those very people hit him with hostility [during the early days of his call to Islam]. And despite being threatened in his own house, he did not commence his grand emigration [from Mecca to Madinah] before returning his consignments [to his rivals], with the risk involved in this action, exposing his intention to depart and hindering his plan to save himself. This adds to his reputation in his youth, as he was used to be called the trustworthy before being called to proclaim the mission that warranted such quality.

All, but actually some, of these qualifications suffice to provide whoever possesses them with the perfect means of friendship and make him loving to his circle and equally entitled to others' love and loyalty. For it has never been the case in the history of the greats, including prophets and non-prophets, that a man won a variety of friendships despite the difference in ranks, environments, attitude, and race, like Prophet Muhammad. And it has never been the case that a man was loved by the hearts of both the weak and strong people like Muhammad in his big heart. We recall the story of Zaid Ibn Harithah – who was kidnapped as a child – and then his father found him in Mecca after a long time and despair, but when he had to choose between his father and his master [Muhammad, PBUH], he preferred to stay with Muhammad over being united with his father, as it was difficult for him to leave the big heart that showered him with his love and comfort when he [Zaid] was the weak and stranger who did not see his family or know who they were.

And it was not enough for those who loved the Prophet to accompany him in this life until they are assured of his company in the hereafter. His servant Thawban looked weak and faint with day and night distress. When his kind master [the Prophet, PBUH] asked him, he said: "I miss you greatly when I do not see you. And I then remembered the hereafter where I will not be able to see you, as you will be in your rank with other prophets." And this story was narrated to be the reason for the verse that was later revealed: *"All who obey Allah and the messenger are in the company of those on whom is the Grace of Allah- of the prophets (who teach), the sincere (lovers of Truth), the witnesses (who testify), and the Righteous (who do good): Ah! What a beautiful fellowship! – Quran, 4:69."*

And at the time of Bilal's[31] death, his family were around him weeping and crying: "What a sorrow!" While he was answering them "What a joy! I will see my beloved ones tomorrow: Muhammad and his companions."

What we meant from the above is to reflect on the friendship that develops between a human being and another human being, not the love between a believer and his Prophet. For the latter was so overwhelming in the hearts of Muslim men and women that a woman heard the news of a battle and that her family members were killed but she was still not distracted from asking about the safety of the Prophet before her immediate family. But what we meant, in fact, is that affection and trust that drove numerous people to believe in Muhammad, as this element was there in their hearts and souls before loving him for the faith and belief.

[31] Translator: One of the Prophet's companion who was a slave but later freed in Islam

THE BEST OF GREATNESS

The kindliness of a great person toward his subordinates with that much love is a virtue of the greatness as humans could ever experience it, [and those subordinates will certainly readily admire this greatness]. However, it could be argued that admiration of the great person by other great individuals is another dimension that is much more valuable and more indicative of the enormous share of the virtues of excellence and superiority of that great person. And this is no doubt true, for Muhammad's miracle also accommodated this side in a manner that could not be matched by any other person who possessed the best types of friendship. For Muhammad (PBUH) was surrounded by an elite band of high caliber who combined the greatness of decent, greatness of wealth, greatness of intellect, and greatness of resolution. And the greatness of each of those individuals within the Prophet's circle was sufficient to nourish a state and support a nation, in the manner that was historically revealed later by the biography of the likes of Abu-Bakr, Umar, Khalid, Usama, Ibn Al-Aas, Al-Zubayr, Talha, and the rest of the first companions.

But a man could be great in only one trait that makes him surrounded by friends and followers who enjoy this trait in the manner the philosophers surrounded Socrates and war generals surrounded Napoléon. It could even be that the righteous surround a great Prophet like the Apostles surrounded Jesus, and they were all of the same background and same environment. Yet the best of greatness is the one that attracts talented individuals from various fields and patterns. And it is the one that would attract people of different personalities, such as Abu-Bakr versus Ali; Umar versus Othman; Khalid versus Muaaz; and Othman versus Ibn Al-Aas. Each one of them is great on his own, although they would disagree on the exact definition of the meaning of greatness.

This is the greatness that expanded in its vastness and diversified in its pattern to the extent that it included all contrasts and possessed a focal point that attracts every talent, combining power and tolerance, directness and maneuver, genius and hard work, and experience of the elders and zeal of the youths. These are undoubtedly the best of greatness and the miracle of the miracles regarding friendship. And Muhammad (PBUH) did not earn this except via a soul rich in love where he nourished this love sincerely and matched every loving person in measure: kindness with kindness and sincerity with sincerity, plus his bit of superfluity that derived from his status and rank.

Prophet Muhammad was the one who conferred on his companions the guidance to the light of the mind and soul, and these are more honorable than the light of the sight, since the latter is shared by humans and animals, whereas the light of the mind and soul are exclusive to humans. Despite that [i.e. his conferral on his companions], he used to remember their virtue and acts, as he said about Abu Bakr: "There is no one that I owe him as much as I owe Abu Bakr; he supported me with his money and soul and let me marry his daughter [Aishah]." He said about Abu Bakr and Umar: "The status of Abu Bakr and Umar is like my sighting and hearing." He said about Ali: "Ali is my brother in this life and in the hereafter." He said about some of his companions: "Allah, glory be to Him, ordered me to love four and informed me that He loves them: Ali, Abu Zarr, Al-Miqdad and Salman." He said about the whole of the Helpers (Al-Ansaar): "Take care and do well to the Helpers: they are my confidants that I took refuge in, be kind to their kids, and forgive the erroneous of them." And he said much more of the same about his companions in general and with specific names.

Yet we can appreciate this big heart and this comprehensive human kindness in the way he treated his enemies and rivals beyond his treatment to his beloved ones or others to whom he had neither affection nor hatred. For he never retaliated from anyone who targeted him personally. And he forgave the man who raised the sword to kill him while asleep before the sword fell away involuntarily. And he never launched a war against anyone when there is a room to avoid it or a means to hold a protective peace with him. And his way of treating Abdullah Ibn Ubay [in Madinah after emigration], whom Muslims used to call the head of hypocrites, is a striking example of the way he overlooked others' mistakes and exercised gracious forgiveness. For Abdullah Ibn Ubay entered a pact, but breached it and he lived his life plotting against the Prophet and supporting his enemies. And the news spread that the Prophet marked him for death, so his son [Abdullah Ibn Abdullah Ibn Ubay] went to the Prophet saying: "Oh Prophet of Allah: I have heard that you have marked Abullah Ibn Ubay for death for what he did. If you are going ahead with this, order me to do it, and I will bring you his head. For by Allah, no one in the clan of Khazragh is known to be as dutiful as I am to his father, and I fear if you order someone else to kill him that I cannot see my father's killer walking alive and that I would kill him. And in this case, I would have killed a believer for a disbeliever and go to the hellfire."

But the Prophet refused to kill his father and opted to treat him gently. [When the father died naturally], the prophet added to his kindness and generosity to the son by offering his garment for the coffin and leading the prayers; the Prophet also spent some time on the father's grave during burial. Umar tried to stop the Prophet from the prayer for the enemy who tried hard to harm him and mentioned the Quranic verse: "*Whether you ask for their forgiveness, or not [i.e. the hypocrites]: if you ask seventy times for their forgiveness, Allah will not forgive them - Quran, 9:80.*" But the Prophet said: "If I know that he would be forgiven if I ask more than seventy times I would."

It is hard to believe that such soul that is naturally marked by friendship, mercy, and tolerance could ever be accused of the cruelty claimed by some of the European historians! How difficult it is for such soul to be accused of cruelty because it penalized some people with death, the same way a judge convicts a criminal of his act, and still remains [the judge] amongst the most merciful humans?

How strange of them to remember the penalty and forget the crime that mandated the penalty, the same way a cause produces an effect! And what crime! It is a crime that if one other than Muhammad handled, he would have shed rivers of blood in his capacity from this worldly life and the hereafter. Let us not forget how the disbelievers ridiculed the Prophet, harassed him, threw the dirt and stone on him, conspired to kill him and his companions, and drove Muslims afar out of their homes. And let us not forget the stubbornness, cunning, and incitement they exercised for no reason, except that they [Muslims] called for worshipping Allah, earning good manners, abandoning idols, and refraining from wickedness.

We will not document herein all of the incidents that fall under the description above, since it is beyond the scope of this book. But we mention one single incident that uniquely included all types of sordidness; this is the tragedy of the forty messengers (seventy in some narrations), who were killed in Be'ar Maaouna[32]. Those messengers did not commit a crime, except that they answered a voluntary call from those who asked for some teachers of Quran and religion. In a tragedy like this, what would these civilized states [of today] do with the treacherous

[32] Translator: A place

had those forty or seventy victims were Christian missionaries killed by a barbaric tribe that eats humans [in this case such tribe could be excused, since they are animal-like creatures]? In the aftermath of the revenge, you may find it difficult to find anyone left alive from this tribe to tell what happened to this people [i.e. the tribe will be destroyed completely in the revenge]. And in this case, those who have retaliated may still be considered merciful in their response!

Yet the tragedy of Be'ar Maaouna was not the only incident of assassination of innocent messengers. We may conclude this chapter about friendship by referring to the treachery of the clan of Huzail when they assassinated the six messengers that went to teach Islam, with no compulsion or wrongdoing. Yet they were all killed! And one of them [named Zaid] was taken as a prisoner and sold to Safwan Ibn Ummaya [from Quraysh, the enemy of Muslims at the time] to kill him for his father. While he was being prepared for the kill, Abu Sufyan asked him sarcastically: "I ask you by Allah Zaid. Would you prefer that Muhammad is in your place while you are safe in your house?" And Zaid replied: "By Allah, I do not like for Muhammad in his safe place to be harmed by a small thorn while I am safe in my family." Abu Sufyan then shouted: "I have never seen someone liked by his companions as Muhammad."

From a situation like this, we learn how much love Muhammad deserved from his companions and how much punishment his enemies deserved. For he loved his companions and was loved by them because he was made for friendship. But for his enemies, they merely got what they deserved because they were made for hostility and animosity.

CHAPTER 8: MUHAMMAD, THE CHIEF

IT IS USEFUL TO WRITE ABOUT MUHAMMAD: the chief, after writing about Muhammad: the friend. For he gave the chieftaincy the meaning of voluntary friendship, as he was the best friend to his subordinates, despite his entitlement to assume all facets of power.

There is a style of ruling by the power of life, and there is a style of ruling by the power of the hereafter, and there is a style of ruling by the power of majesty and competency. In this regard, Muhammad (PBUH) had the right ownership: in terms of the power of life, he had absolute control over his people; in terms of the power of the hereafter, he had all of what prophets knew about the unseen beyond what the general public see and perceive; and in terms of the power of majesty and competency, he possessed the traits that were acknowledged by his followers to make him both the best capable and the most noble person. Yet he voluntarily opted to be the greatest chief by the power of the great friendship, the power of love, satisfaction, and choice.

[This style of ruling was manifested in many ways]. He was the man who consulted men the most, and love was his condition for someone to rule or lead the prayers, as he said: "The prayer of the disliked leader will not be accepted." And he used to commit himself with what the most humble of his followers is committed with. It is narrated that he was on a journey and asked his companions to prepare a lamb: a man said, "I will slaughter it"; another one said, "I will skin it"; a third man said, "I will cook it." The Prophet (PBUH) said: "And I will collect the wood." They said: "Oh Prophet, we take care of this for you." He said: "I know you can, but I hate to be seen as special, for Allah hates to see his servant treated preferably among his companions."

And when Muslims were digging the ditch [for the Battle of the Combined Forces], he insisted on working by his hands with them. And if it were not that he wished to give examples to chiefs that they must endure responsibilities, he would have exempted himself from the work and his companions would have happily exempted him.

He rendered helping others to fulfil their needs a means to Allah's pardon, saying: "Allah has chosen certain people to help others, and people go to them at the time of need. Those are the ones that will be safe from Allah's punishment."

And he was the most learned about the fact that deeds are acts of the intention, but he also learned that when a ruler treats his people suspiciously, he ruins them. Accordingly, he did not pursue peoples' intentions, leaving this to Allah, and he opted to treat people by what they can be accounted for.

He heard a dispute [between two people asking for the Prophet's ruling] outside his house. He went out and said: "I am a human being; one of you may be more fluent in putting his case before me than the other, and I would believe him accordingly. So, anyone I rule in his favour wrongly at the expense of a Muslim's right, it is as if I cut him a piece of fire. Let him then take it or leave it."

Nowadays, people argue about the freedom of thought, considering it to be one of the discoveries of the French Revolution and beyond. And in this, they dictate that the ruler cannot penalize people for what they think of them [i.e. in silence], as long as they do not speak out or act on something that violates the law. However, what they consider as a discovery of the 19th century was implemented and legislated by the Prophet some 14 centuries ago for his nation when he said: "Allah has forgiven my nation for what they think of themselves, so long as they do not act upon it or speak of it."

They also claimed that prioritizing mercy over justice in applying the law is an unprecedented call made by the modernists, whereas it is the very same call that the Arab Prophet repeated and never called otherwise. He said: "When Allah decreed the creation, He pledged Himself by writing: my mercy prevails over my wrath." And he said: "Allah is kind and likes kindness and reward for it what he would not reward over roughness." And he said: "Allah glory be to him did not send me as rigid or stubborn, but he sent me as a teacher and facilitator." His companions narrated that he was never given a choice between two matters, but he chose the easier, unless it violated the religion.

He used to advise that the weaklings should be taken care of. And he said to his companions: “Be kind to the weaklings, for you are not provided and supported but through your weaklings.” And he denounced arrogance with servants and poor people. In this regard, he did not disdain eating with his servants, he rode donkeys in the marketplace, and tied sheep and milked them. Nevertheless, with his mercy toward the youngsters, he did not ignore the right of the elderly and seniors: “Whoever does not show mercy to the youngsters and acknowledge the right of the elderly [seniors] is not one of us.” For fairness is not disallowed for the elderly and allowed only for the youngsters, as each side has a right and a share. Respecting people for their status was his practice, as he advised his people. And all of the above are the best guidelines to run a state successfully, and without these, nations would actually demise.

The chief Prophet learned that chieftaincy is for all subordinates, not only for the ones who gave consent or approval. Therefore, he advised his people: “Fear the supplication of the aggrieved, even from a disbeliever, since it ascends [to heaven] uninterrupted.” And when a person who is both a prophet and a chief says that, it is then the best tradition to be followed by all chiefs, since they are not sent to proclaim religion and eradicate blasphemy as prophets did.

Muhammad’s way of practicing chieftaincy was through friendship; and accordingly, if someone relied less on Sharia’a (law), [i.e. in favour of friendship] in this regard, it is for sure Muhammad, notwithstanding he is the one who brought this Sharia'a to his followers.

CHAPTER 9: THE HUSBAND

SPEAKING OF A HUSBAND ENTAILS talking about the status of women as seen by men and the status of women in general as perceived by men in general. The status women have achieved thanks to Muhammad and his religion could be appreciated when one appreciates the status of women in the era before Islam, in the era of Islam and beyond and also in non-Arab nations.

Two main aspects can be invoked to show the huge difference between the women status before and after Islam. Before Islam, woman was an inheritable property to be distributed among heirs like a cattle. But thanks to Islam and the Prophet, she has been given rights, she has inherited and made to be inherited, and she has been assured that marriage does not prevent her from controlling her own wealth.

And woman was a disgrace that must be buried alive to avoid her shame; or she was seen as a financial liability that must be buried in her babyhood; but she has now become [in Islam] a valuable human being protected against any harm.

In non-Arab countries, the situation was not any better because women were enslaved in Romans' laws. Women were deemed impure at the beginning of Christianity. And it is striking to describe the women status in the knighthood era, which was described as being the golden time for women in the European nations and that knights used to redeem women with blood and wealth. This era was actually an era of the horse rather than being the era of woman or the 'redeemed lady', which was described by John Langdon-Davies [1897-1971] in his book, "A Short History of Women." He said: "It was known during the knighthood age that youths generally lost interest in the opposite sex. But this should not be surprising when we recall, contrary to what others may think, that 'knighthood' had nothing to do with women, but had everything to do with horses. For the interest in women never matched the interest in horses, except as being a productive asset."

The reader may refer to a conversation from the book "Song of Deeds." In it is a story that Auseis's daughter sat one day by her window and was seen by two youths, Garran and Gerbert. Garran said: "Look Gerbert: I swear on the Virgin Mary, she is a beautiful girl," without looking at him! And he then went back saying: "I do not think I have ever seen a beautiful girl like this; how beautiful these two black eyes are!" They then left while Gerbert was saying: "I do not think there is a horse like that horse [referring to the girl]!" Although this is a small story, it is actually very meaningful, for carelessness leads to contempt. And the reality is that the knighthood presented some clear evidences of this contempt.

Here is another story in the book above. It says that Queen Blancheflour went to see her counterpart King Pepin asking him to support the people of Lorraine. The king listened to her and suddenly got outraged and slapped her on the nose with his full hand; four drops of blood fell [off her nose]. She then cried: "Thank you, if this has made you pleased with me, slap me one more time whenever you wish." And this was not a one off story because numerous words of the same nature flow in the book as a memorized formula. As if the slap by the hand was the punishment received by any woman that directs an advice to her husband.

"...and it was the norm that a woman gets married to a man within hours, and in many cases she may get married to someone whom she had never seen, either for the sake of military alliance and support or for facilitating a deal regarding lands. And it was the norm for a woman married to a knight to be mad about wars, but lacking intelligence and illiterate in most cases, to be bashed every time she makes a mistake. It is no wonder then that the queen of the palace did not find mercy or shelter from the misery or the compulsion to get married to someone who is not a match."

However, even after the dark ages in the West, delving into the knighthood era to the beginnings of the modern history, the status of woman in the West was low, even worse than her status in the pre-Islamic Arab region. For example, two women were sold in England's market for two Shillings, because the Church responsible for them was burdened by the cost of their living.

Furthermore, women did not have the right to own properties or lodge lawsuits until 1882.

Woman's education was a shame to be abhorred by women, let alone men. During her education at Geneva University in 1849, Elizabeth Blackwell – the first female physician in the world – was antagonized and evaded by the women she lived with. They also used to collect their skirts away from touching her to avoid impurity.

And when a group of people managed later to establish a medical institute for women in Philadelphia (USA), the medical community announced rejection of any doctor who get educated in this institute and any patient who seeks treatment there.

While the West advanced at the beginning of our modern history, the status of women did not improve beyond the slavery that plagued Arab women pre-Islam.

So what did Muhammad do? And what did his mission achieve?

One single ruling from Quran established the rights and obligations of women: "*And women shall have rights similar to the rights against them, according to what is equitable – Quran, 2:228.*"

And in another noble ruling, Islam commanded the husband to treat his wife kindly, even if he dislikes her: "*Live with them on a footing of kindness and equity. If you take a dislike to them, it may be that you dislike a thing, and Allah brings about through it a great deal of good – Quran, 4:19.*"

Islam also gave women the rights to inherit as men do: "*From what is left by parents and those nearest related there is a share for men and a share for women, whether the property be small or large,-a determinate share – Quran, 4:32.*" And Islam has not granted man any preference except in the course of assigning him the responsibility to provide and take care of her. Furthermore, Muhammad (PBUH) rendered that the best of Muslims are those who are best [in treating] to their wives, "The most complete of the believers in faith are those with the best character, and the best of you are the best in behavior to their women."

And he commanded men to manage the woman' weakness and shortcomings intelligently: "Act kindly toward women, for they were created from a rib, and the most crooked part of a rib is its uppermost. If you attempt to straighten it; you will break it, and if you leave it alone it will remain crooked; so act kindly toward women."

He advised that man should beautify himself and appear in the best form for his wife. So he said (PBUH): "Wash your clothes and trim the excess hair on your bodies and brush your teeth and beautify yourselves and keep yourselves clean, since certainly the Children of Israel never did these things and thus, their women committed adultery." And he advised that: "If someone asks a woman for marriage while he dies his hair black, he must inform her that he dies."

And he cared about respecting a woman's feeling and accommodating her natural shyness to the extent that he advised the husband to care for her pleasure as he cares for himself, as she may not explicitly ask him for what he asks of her: "When the husband has sexual intercourse with his wife, he must not stop once he fulfils his pleasure, but must be patient until she fulfils hers."

And the way he educated Muslims in this regard was so wise and intelligent: "If you are entering your home from a long travel, do not enter by night, but let your wives know of your arrival to clean themselves and coif: intelligence, intelligence!"

HIS TREATMENT TO HIS WIVES

What the Prophet advised Muslims as to how they should treat their wives is much less than what he ordained on himself in this regard toward his own wives. For he cared that they must see him smiley and used to visit them all in the morning and evening. And when in seclusion with them, he was: "The softest, smiling, and laughing", as his wife Aishah said.

And he did not render the status of his prophethood a barrier between him and his wives. Rather, he made them, via his leniency and company, to occasionally forget that they were dealing with the Messenger of Allah. And one of them said once to the Prophet in front of her father: "Say, but mention only the truth..." And one of them used to argue with him and avoid him for a whole day. And they were sometimes so daring that when Umar heard about that he was shocked and intended to smack his daughter Hafsa [the Prophet's wife], fearing that she may be doing the same. And when the Prophet saw his anger, he quietened him and said: "We have not invited you to do this." And he used to do housework with them, saying: "Serving your wife is a good deed."

He used to ask Allah's forgiveness for things he had no control over and could not share among his wives equally; that is his heart inclination: "Oh Allah, this is how I treat them equally in what I can control; so do not blame me for what I cannot control."

And when the death illness hit and prevented him from visiting his wives daily as he used to do, he sent to ask them gently: "Where am I tomorrow? Where am I tomorrow?" So that they answer: "With Aishah" and give him permission to stay in her room, although he was entitled in his illness to stay wherever he liked, blamelessly.

Dealing with others nicely over a long period is a rare virtue among humans, although it could readily be understood. Yet the difficult thing to understand is the kind treatment when the marriage is threatened in the most serious aspect, i.e. faithfulness. In this case, no matter how far the modern civilization rises, it can never dream of a treatment kinder and more dignified than that offered by the Prophet in the incident (the Slander Affair) of Aisha, the daughter of Al-Siddiq [Abu Bakr], while she was the dearest of his wives. And the story is as follows.

[In a trip with the Prophet], Aishah went out some distance from the camp to attend to the call of nature. When she returned, she discovered that she had dropped her necklace somewhere. The necklace itself was of no great value, but as it was a loan from a friend, Aishah went out again to search for it. On her return, to her great grief and mortification, the army had already marched away with the camel she was riding; her attendants thought that she was in the litter as she was then thin, very young, and light in weight. In her helplessness, she sat down and cried till sleep overpowered her. Safwan Ibn Mu'attal, an Emigrant, who was coming in the rear recognized her as he had seen her before the verse enjoining the veil was revealed, and brought her on his camel to Madinah without saying a single word to her, himself walking behind the animal. The hypocrites of Madinah led by Abdullah Ibn Ubay Ibn Salul, sought to make capital out of this incident and spread a malicious scandal against Aishah, and unfortunately, some of the Muslims also became involved.

On arrival in Madinah, the Prophet (PBUH) held counsel with his companions [about the matter], who pronounced different opinions ranging from divorce to retention [of his wife Aishah].

The incident almost raised a fight between two [old] rival factions, Al-Aws and Al-Khazraj, but the Prophet's intervention silenced both parties on the spot. Aishah, unaware of the rumors being circulated, fell ill and was confined to bed for a month. On recovering, she heard of the slander and took permission to go and see her parents seeking authentic news. She then burst into tears and stayed for two days and one sleepless night ceaselessly weeping to such an extent that she felt her liver was about to rip open. The Prophet (PBUH) visited her in that situation, and after testifying to the Oneness of Allah he told her, "If you are innocent, Allah will acquit you, otherwise, you have to beg for His forgiveness and pardon." She stopped weeping and asked her parents to speak for her, but they had nothing to say, so she herself took the initiative and said: "Should I tell you I am innocent, and Allah knows that I am surely innocent, you will not believe me; and if I were to admit something of which Allah knows I am innocent, you will believe me, then I will have nothing to make recourse to except the words of the father of Prophet Yusuf (Joseph): "*So (for me) patience is most fitting. And it is Allah (Alone) Whose Help can be sought against that which you assert – Quran, 12:18.*" She then turned away and lay down for some rest. At that decisive moment, the revelation came acquitting Aishah of all the slanderous talk fabricated in this concern. Aishah of course, was wholeheartedly joyful and praised Allah thankfully. Allah's words in this regard went as follows: "*Verily! Those who brought forth the slander (against Aishah) are a group among you – Quran, 24-11.*"

This is the story known as the 'Slander Affair' as narrated by Lady Aishah; and it is a highly useful event to explore the tenderness and chivalry in the way the Prophet used to treat his wives, such traits could be missing in many others. For the Prophet in this situation is not facing an event that he can simply be content with to exhibit his natural character of tenderness and patience. It is rather a situation that invites rage, love, bitterness, and may oppose every urge for good treatment. Yet the reaction of the Prophet was pure nobleness in the way he acted toward himself, his wife, and his religion. And in acting this way, he did not leave the best dreamer of the modern civilization to match him in all respects. For the Prophet heard slander being circulated by the hypocrites and it reached Muslims and the closest circle of the Prophet. And it was so serious that someone like Ali Ibn Abi Taleb advised the Prophet to divorce Aishah, saying: "There are many other women around," although Ali was known to be dutiful and naturally kind and generous.

The Prophet heard this evil talk [the slander] but he did not accept it without evidence, neither did he discard it without evidence. And he had to either check on his ill wife or ignore her for a while. But he opted to visit her, while his kindness and fairness prevented him from asking her about the issue that is hurting him while she was ill. But at the same time, he was so emotional and anxious about the issue that he was not able to be entirely normal in the way he used to treat her. And he kept asking about her in a manner that reflects his disappointment and anxiety for her recovery to get the full truth, which will result in him getting either tougher or more compassionate. And in his way of handling that painful situation, he was not deterred by the hastening noise made by people around him to take the right action that fits both kindness and manhood simultaneously.

He asked his confidants: Ali and Usama, who were like his sons. And he asked the female servant Baraira who knew Aishah and also faithful to her master [i.e. the Prophet]. He also asked her fellow wife Zainab Bint Gahsh who was closely dear to him like Aishah, and she would have been the first to tell if she knew something sinister; but she said: "I protect my sighting and hearing. By Allah, I do not know except good [about Aishah]."

And he talked to Aishah when she asked for his permission to visit her family after knowing about the slander, and he was avoiding talking to her before then, holding the bitter issue in his chest, fearing that he may hurt her in her illness if he raises the matter. He raised the issue now so that she either declares her innocence or asks for forgiveness. Aishah was angered like any innocent when unfairly suspected. And she was indeed innocent when seen by any rational person who can understand that a woman like Aishah would not trouble herself in front of the whole army, in daylight, unnecessarily, and with a Muslim man who fears in a situation like this to anger the Prophet, Muslims, and Allah. For this is a sordid act that others would rise above, even if they are less than Aishah in background, status, and pride. And someone like Aishah in her known position and status would refrain from such act. Yet the Prophet wanted to reveal her innocence in front of everyone and himself, ensuring that her innocence should not be merely drawn from his love to her or her general weakness rather than being drawn from investigation and evidence. And once he exhausted all aspects and evidently regained confidence, he then gathered all elements of kindness, manhood, fairness and compassion, all combined.

Indeed he was merciful even with those argumentative individuals who circulated this slander around; and what type of mercy is this when someone forgives those who lie about the reputation of his family, the happiness of his house, and the security of his private life? While in fact, people will not excuse anyone [if he penalizes the perpetrators] as they would excuse an obeyed Prophet who is falsely accused in his honor and then justly punish the perpetrator.

FORBEARANCE OF THE GENEROUS MAN

We knew from various narrations that Abdullah Ibn Ubay Ibn Salul was the most involved in the slander affair out of evil intention and cunning against the Prophet and his faith. And, as indicated above, this man was disliked by Muslims, untrustworthy, and suspected. They used to call him the head of the hypocrites, and reiterated to the Prophet that he should mark him for death. Accordingly, it was easy for the Prophet to let Muslims punish him for the lies, plotting, and attack on the Prophet's honor to stop his evil and make him an example. And if someone says that Abdullah Ibn Ubay had strong clan to be feared [if the prophet punishes him], how about Mostah[33] who was supported by Abu Bakr who used to provide for him from his own wealth; what saved Mostah from the punishment and guaranteed for him future duty and support, except the generosity and kindness of the Prophet, generosity and kindness of Abu Bakr, and generosity and kindness of the Quran?

Yet the clan that Abdullah Ibn Ubay could have taken refuge in would not have really availed him if the Prophet actually wanted to punish him, even with the harshest penalty. For there is nothing stronger in loyalty than the connection between a son known for his dutifulness and his father. This is the same son who volunteered to kill his father when he heard that the Prophet had marked him for death. But in fact, it was the generosity and kindness [of the Prophet that drove towards amnesty].

It was indeed the generosity and kindness that embraced Mostah as it embraced the head of the hypocrites, emerging from the whole affair of the slander with values of forgiveness for all the sinners, the sincere of them, and the insincere. And the whole event unveiled the best treatment for a wife in the most serious

---

33 Translator: One of the Muslims who spread the slander affair

and critical situation, and this is indeed the noblest example to follow. It is a way of treatment that was steady, consistent, and invariant not only over days or months, but it rather lasted over the years, not with one woman but with different ones [i.e. wives of the Prophet]. And the Prophet's treatment to his wives lasted in all circumstances, including the most painful, and was never limited to the condition of happiness and tranquility. This way of treatment surpasses the best wish for those dreaming for a lasting affection between wives and husbands today in what is called the woman era, in which people strive to improve the women status to an unprecedented level.

POLYGAMY

Here we talk about the marriages of the Prophet, which is the second target most aimed at by the defamers of Islam. They keep hitting this target when they talk about the character of the Prophet (PBUH) and refer to this as being out of character for prophets who [are supposed to] provide guidance for people's souls.

The sword and women! As if they wanted to depict the Prophet as someone who submits himself to anger and lust, which are both non-existent in prophets.

The issue of the sword was covered previously.

As for women, the accusation is weaker than the charge regarding sword. For submission to the desire is the last thing that a rational analyst – Muslim or non-Muslim – can think of upon investigation of the marriages of the Prophet in what this really indicate and the associated justification.

Some of the orientalists claim that nine wives is a proof that the Prophet was oversexed. We respond that if you cannot accuse Jesus Christ of being undersexed since he never married; equally you should not describe Muhammad as being oversexed because he had nine wives.

Before we add to this topic, let us establish that there is no issue for a great man to love women and enjoy them, for this is natural. And no instinct is stronger among living creatures than the sexual desire and the male-female sexual relationship. It is the instinct that inspires every living being more than any other instinct in all aspects of life. Have you seen the fish travelling thousands of miles crossing salty water into a hole in sweet water to lay eggs and resume life before travelling the same distance back? Have you seen the bird building its nest and travel back from its migration journey to its home? Have you seen the flowers open up to tempt bees and birds to transport its pollen? Have you seen the life instinct in every living being? What else could it be other than the affection between the opposite sexes? And where the natural instinct would be if it is not in this direction?

So, love for women is not a fault, for this is undoubtedly the natural instinct. The fault is when this love gets out of control and distracts the person from his goals and requires extremism to fulfil it. In this case, it is a twist of the instinct that must be blamed the same way any eccentricity is blamed in all other manners. [The fact is that] no one really understands what the Prophet did and achieved in his life and still thinks that women diverted him from pursuing a small or a big goal of his.

For who amongst those who made history in his life and after his death achieved what Muhammad's call and the Muslim nation achieved? And who can claim that this could ever be the achievement of someone who was occupied by women? Instead, one should ask: in what did women occupy him? And who was ever dedicated to achieving something and then achieved it in the way Muhammad did for his cause?

For if the greatness of the man [Muhammad] empowered him to give justice to his call and fairness to women, this adds to his greatness and does not take from it. And this sounds like completeness [in his personality] and superiority rather than a fault.

And it is utterly strange to claim that the Prophet succumbed to his lust, while he almost divorced his wives and gave them the option to divorce after asking him for more expenditures beyond his means. For they complained – despite their pride in being associated with him – that they do not have enough resources for spending and cosmetics. They all united on this request relentlessly until the Prophet became gloomed with silence and decided to offer them the option either to divorce or live within his financial limitations.

Abu Bakr tried to visit him once, but he found many people standing by his door waiting for permission. Abu Bakr and Umar then entered and found the Prophet surrounded by his wives, gloomed, and in silence. Abu Bakr wanted to say something funny to ease him: "Oh Messenger of Allah, if you could have seen the daughter of Khareja [Abu Bakr's wife] asked me for more provisions. I stood up and smacked her head." The Prophet laughed and said: "Here they are around me asking for the same." Abu Bakr jumped on Aishah to smack her, and Umar did the same with his daughter Hafsa, saying: "Do you ask the Prophet beyond his means?" They said: "By Allah, we never ask him beyond his means."

The Prophet then left his wives for a month until the Quranic verse that offered them the option to choose between him and the resources was revealed: "*Oh Prophet, tell your wives: If you seek the world and its embellishments, then come and I will make some provision for you and release you in an honorable way. But if you seek Allah and His Messenger and the abode of the Hereafter, then surely Allah has prepared a great reward for those of you who do good – Quran, 33:28-29.*"

The Prophet then started with Aishah saying: "Aishah I wish to ask you something but I do not want you to hasten the decision before you talk to your parents." She said: "What is it Oh

Messenger of Allah?" And he recited the Quranic verses. She said: "I do not need to consult my parents about you Oh Messenger of Allah?" I would rather choose Allah and His Messenger and the Abode of the Hereafter." And he did the same with the rest of his wives, and they answered like Aishah and accepted their tight living conditions that were much inferior to those of many other ordinary Muslims.

What can we make of this? Muhammad's wives complain from the tight living conditions and lack of embellishment. Had he willed, he could have showered them with prosperity and immersed them in silk, gold, and best food. Is this an act of someone who succumbed to his lust?

Was it not easy for him to allocate himself and his wives from booties and spoils of wars in measures that make them happy while not upsetting Muslims at the same time, as they [Muslims] know that the will of the Prophet draws from the will of Allah?

And what did he had to violate to keep his wives so that one may claim that he was excessive in his desire for women? Did this cost him to violate his noble traditions, deviate from what could abase his reputation, or compromise on something that can still be accepted by his followers?

Muhammad compromised none of the above! And his marriages did not distract him from his biggest or tiniest goals. We did not see in his biography a man who was defeated by his lust as his rivals claim. On the contrary! We saw a man overcoming the pleasure of food, living, and women, and controlling himself while not accepting any imposition, even if it is a provision of extra resources that a humble Muslim would normally attain, despite his capacity to achieve this had he willed.

A MAN OF SERIOUSNESS AND COMPOSURE

This is how we examine the biography of the man who his rivals from the European historians portrayed, but all we see is the worst delusion [of those historians] that one can imagine. For we see a man who could have lived like a king had he wanted, but he chose to live poor. And despite that, he was accused of being defeated by his lust!

And we see a man whose wives are revolting because he did not provide them with the resources to beautify for him. And despite that, he was accused of being defeated by his lust!

And we see a man who opted to live on basic necessities and preferred to remain content with his limitations over pleasing his wives with something that was within his reach. And despite, that he was accused of being defeated by his lust!

This is the claim that could be rendered as the funniest joke that the defamers would be very successful at if they wanted to joke. But this would be the worst success!

And the thing that is even stranger about this claim is that the man they deluded about was not unknown before or after his marriage, for them to be confused so remarkably. For

Muhammad's youth was well known before the onset of his Islamic mission, the best a young man would be known in the entire of Quraysh and Mecca.

He was known from his young age to his old age. He was never known to have succumbed to his pleasure needs in his youth. And he was never known to have played like other young men when the life pre-Islam was permissive. He was rather known to be a pure, honest, serious, and composed person. And when he started his call afterward, none of his haters, critics or those who were digging beyond him said: "Hey, see this man who used to do such and such with women in his youth, he is now calling for purity, chastity, and abandoning desires." Ney, none of those said that about him, although they were huge in number. And if this had the tiniest truth [about a stained past of the Prophet], thousands would have echoed it.

When he married his first wife [before Islam], Khadijah, it was not his lust that dictated this marriage, because when he did she was about 40 years old and he was about 25 years old. And [after her death], he remained unmarried until his 50s, with no urge to marry to another woman. And his loyalty to her the rest of his life [after her death] was not for sure driven by his lust or memories of life enjoyment. Because he chose her over the young Aishah, who was later the dearest to him among his other wives. And Aishah used to feel jealous of Khadija, even in her grave. Actually, the Prophet never hid from Aishah that Khadija was his dearest. Aishah said to him once: "She [Khadija] was merely an old woman that Allah compensated you with better than her." He replied angrily: "No by Allah, Allah did not compensate me with anything better than her. She accepted the faith when people rejected, believed me when people belied me, supported me with her wealth when people deprived me, and Allah blessed me with children only from her and not from other women." For these reasons, he loved Khadija and preferred her, and none of her fellow women after her erased his memories of her. This is a loyalty of the heart, not a self-pleasure nor a memory of life enjoyment.

REASONS FOR HIS SEVERAL MARRIAGES

And if sexual desire is what drove the Prophet toward marriage after Khadija's death, it would have been more satisfactory to this desire had he combined nine of the most beautiful virgin women known across Mecca, Madinah and the whole of the Arab Peninsula. And one would expect these nine girls to accept swiftly with pride, and their parents to be more accepting and prouder with this unmatched marriage. But instead, he never married a virgin other than Aisha. However, his marriage from Aishah was not initially intended until a lady named Khawla Bint Hakim mentioned her to the Prophet after Khadija had died. Aishah said: "After Khadija had died, Khawla Bint Hakim, the wife of Othman Ibn Mazoun said to the Prophet: "Oh Messenger of Allah, why do not you marry?" He said: "From who?" She said:

"A virgin or non-virgin if you like." He said: "Who is the virgin?" She said: "The daughter of the most beloved man to you, Aishah the daughter of Abu Bakr." He said: "And who is the non-virgin?" She said: "Sawda Bint Zamaa; she believed in you and followed you."

It was then Sawda, the first woman that the Prophet married after Khadija's death. Her former husband (and cousin) died after coming back from the emigration to Abyssinia. She was among the first women that accepted Islam, and she left her family and migrated with her husband to Abyssinia fleeing the harassment of the polytheists [in Mecca]. After her husband had died, she was left with the scenario of going back to her family to denounce Islam, marry someone who does not match her or find a match who may not be keen on her marriage. The Prophet then married her for protection and reducing the rivalry with her clan. If this was for the sexual desire and enjoyment, the Prophet would have sought a different woman!

The Prophet had another wife, Zainab Bint Gahsh, his cousin. She was known for her beauty and youth. The Prophet arranged for her marriage from Zaid Ibn Harithah [the Prophet's former adopted son]. She was not very happy with this marriage, because she refused haughtily to marry from a freed slave, given the status of her family and her relation to the Prophet. In this case, too, the Prophet was not driven by his desire in marrying from Zainab after Zaid had divorced her and the Prophet could not manage to reconcile them. If the Prophet was indeed driven by desire when he married Zainab, it would have been easier for him to take the step before Zaid and never persuaded her to accept him after her initial rejection. For she was his cousin, and he used to see her since childhood, and nothing of her beauty came as a surprise to him when he strongly recommended Zaid to her for marriage. When the rift between Zaid and Zainab widened after their marriage, and Zaid kept complaining her avoidance, pride, and roughness, the Prophet's marriage to Zainab came as a solution to the problem that haunted his adopted son and the cousin who accepted the marriage based on his advice, but without success[34].

And as for the rest of his wives, there was no single case but associated with a reason involving general benefit [for Islam] or a drive from his kindness and chivalry. For Umm Salama was very old when he asked her for marriage, as she described herself to exempt him when he wanted to appease her after the death of her husband, Abdullah Al-Makhzoumi, from an injury he had during the Battle of Uhud. When she was saddened and heartbroken by the death of her husband, the Prophet consoled her: "Ask Allah to reward you in your calamity and substitute in betterment." And she said: "Who could be better than Abu Salama [her deceased husband]?" The Prophet then ordained

[34] Translator: Quran revealed that the wisdom behind the marriage of the Prophet from Zainab after she was divorced from Zaid was to revoke the tradition of adoption. Reference can be made to Chapter 33.

that he should marry her after knowing that both Abu Bakr and Umar asked for her marriage and she declined, and they were of the highest status among Muslims after the Prophet.

The Prophet's wife, Joayriah Bent Al-Hareth, was the daughter of her clan's chief. She was one of the captives of the Battle of Banu Al-Mustalaq[35]. The Prophet married her and freed her in a move to encourage Muslims to free their captives to relieve them and soften their hearts. The captives accepted Islam and did well in it. And her father gave her the choice to either join him or remain with the Prophet, and she chose the Prophet.

The Prophet's wife, Hafsa Bint Umar Ibn Al-Khattab, was widowed and her father approached Abu Bakr and Othman to marry her, but they both remained silent. Umar expressed his sorrow to the Prophet, who did not wish to grudge the relationship he offered before to Abu Bakr [i.e. alliance by marriage to his daughter Aisha] against Umar, his friend and supporter. He said to Umar: "Hafsa will marry someone better than Abu Bakr and Othman."

The Prophet's wife, Ramla the daughter of Abu Sufyan, left her father for Islam, and abandoned her home place and migrated with her husband to Abyssinia. There, her husband embraced Christianity and estranged her, leaving her without a provider. The Prophet sent to Negus [the King of Ethiopia] to affiance her

[35] Translator: A Jew tribe

for him to save her from loss of home, loss of family, and loss of the partner. Evidently, the marriage in this case was driven by a humanitarian relief rather than pleasure and procurement of more wives. Another noble reason the Prophet had from this marriage, but he did not have it in mind until he was obliged to, is to connect with Abu Sufyan [the chief of Quraysh] via a marriage relationship, in case this guides him to Islam by softening his heart and satisfying his pride.

Other marriages of the Prophet were driven by his tradition in re-dignifying those who got humiliated after esteem, a tradition he followed with all people, especially women whose hearts were broken after losing the protectors and relatives. And this is why he gave Safiyah, the first lady of Banu Qurayzah, the choice to either join her family or be freed and marry him, and she chose him.

Yet the strongest indication of the Prophet's emotional intelligence and care about humans' feelings is that he rebuked his close friend Bilal because he showed Safiyah and her female cousin the dead bodies of the killed Jews, saying angrily: "Was the mercy snatched away from your heart when you let the women see the bodies of their killed people?" And Zainab [his other wife] despised Safiyah once and called her the 'Jew'; the Prophet then abandoned Zainab and did not speak to her for a full month in support and protection of this foreign lady [Safiyah].

Reviewing the marital life of Muhammad (PBUH) reveals some of the good reasons behind his several concurrent marriages, as discussed above.

And as indicated before, there is no harm for someone naturally to seek pleasure in marriage. Yet the pleasure was never the first reason the Prophet considered in any of his marriages, whether before or after his call for Islam, and whether in his youth or old age. And in this regard, the last thing a fair person can think of is the picture of a man [Muhammad] who applied himself to his lust and carefully picked beautiful women one after another based on his pleasure needs. On the contrary, the choices he made in his marriages were driven by the need of his women to an honorable shelter or driven by the benefit in establishing kinship relationship between him and the chiefs and masters of the peninsula, enemies, and friends, for the sake of his grand cause [Islam]. And there is no one single exception from the reasons above in all of his marriages, including his marriage to the beautiful Lady Aishah who was virgin when he married her.

Yet the defamers [of the prophet] forgot every single fact about the Prophet's marital life, which was accurately documented in detail, only to mention one thing they twisted in interpretation to falsely accuse the Prophet because he had nine wives at the same time. They forgot that he was known for his purity and chastity in his youth, as he did not allow himself to indulge in the fun activities that were readily, publicly, and legitimately available to all youths before Islam.

And they [the defamers] forgot that he remained a bachelor until he was 25 years old without seeking the marriage that was available to every handsome, young, well-born man favorable among families and girls [like him].

And they forgot [the defamers] that when he married at the age of 25, he was married to a 40-year-old lady, and he was content with this until she died when he was in his 50s.

And they forgot [the defamers] that he chose to connect in his marriage with women in much need for either care or heart softening, and that he did not choose beauty to satisfy his desire.

And they forgot [the defamers] that the man they described as someone succumbing to his lust used to spend days without enough barley bread to eat and that he was always content with his humble conditions, with no keenness to change these conditions to entertain himself or his wives. And had he willed to go affluent, it would have not cost him much trouble thanks to his capacity and the resources he controlled.

They forgot [the defamers] all of that, although it is well documented, the same way his several concurrent marriages are well documented. So why did they forget it? They forgot because they intended to criticize, invent, and twist the truth, whereas seeing the truth was easier than ignoring it if they really wanted it; and they meant to mention it [the lie] and did not intend to forget it [the lie].

ETHICAL SIDE

We will briefly now discuss Muhammad's polygamy from the ethical and moral side, since the thrust in this book is related to his multifaceted genius, rather than addressing the wisdom of the Islamic Sharia'a in its details and justifications.

The briefest we can say about the polygamy from the ethical and moral side is that the Prophet did not make the polygamy per se something good to chase or to be chosen by someone unnecessarily. Rather, he made it a permission against a necessity that must be acknowledged by man and society, as it can be the most pressing necessity. And no one can deny this element, except those stubborn who reject the truths and ignore the most obvious thing.

For in Muhammad's marital life, no one can deny that his marriages were a shield protecting his women from widowhood, humiliation, and conversion to blasphemy and aberration. And no one can deny that his marriages were better than cutting off the connection that he established with the families and clans, which benefited Islam and Muslims. And these are necessities that will be invariably acknowledged by every leader responsible for a nation, and every leader insightful into people's characters.

On the other hand, the general social necessity [behind polygamy] is also acknowledged by all modern societies, which later detached from this necessity by legalizing adultery and solving the marriage issue with means unrelated to marriage and family values. And had this modern society found a solution better than polygamy, one could then understood the critique of polygamy, which is in fact a more honorable solution than other solutions.

For it is undoubtedly more honorable for the sterile or sick wife as well as the society that the husband marries another woman together with this wife [the sick or sterile] than leaving her struggling in this life without a son, a husband or a protector. Plus, it is honorable for the husband himself who is a living being wishing to connect with life via good offspring, which is the purpose behind every marriage, and without it all reasons for marriage would be futile. There is no doubt that marrying a new woman together with an undesirable wife is more honorable and healthier than bringing together with her a lover or several lovers.

Facilitating polygamy, especially at times of war when the men population drops, is more honorable for the human societies than facilitating other relationships that do not add to the values or human species and do not improve the status of a woman by marriage.

Polgymy then could be something reasonable! And actually it is more than reasonable because it is an inevitable fact that cannot be avoided. And there should not be a blame on someone who can solve the problem [the social side of polygamy] with a solution that is more honorable than other solutions [such as adultery and prostitution]. In fact, the blame is on those who examine the world critically and close their eyes about their very own facts that shock every eye.

It is easy for anyone to manage the world affairs in his imagination with the virtues that he likes and accepts. However, it is not easy for that person to create the actual world that can comply and necessarily accept what he has accepted. And this has been known to everyone confronted with any of the problems that faced Muhammad without a precedence, except through what Allah inspired him [to solve these unprecedented problems].

For what did Napoléon do in our modern era? The reason we consider the case of Napoléon is that he witnessed a revolution on the conditions and traditions [in reference to the French revolution] similar to the changes occurred during the day of Muhammad's mission. And Napoléon also witnessed a deterioration in the ethics and manners akin to that experienced by Arabs toward the end of the pre-Islam era. Plus, Napoléon established a state, considered legislation, and tried to introduce reforms.

Napoléon divorced his wife and forced the church ministers to approve the divorce. And he had numerous affairs with many women, known and unknown. Napoléon said: "I did everything within my capacity to help those poor innocent children of adultery. But you cannot actually do much without compromising marriage rules. Otherwise, most people will abstain from marriage. And man in the old time used to have female slaves for his pleasure besides wives. And the children of adultery were not despised by people like in these days. It is laughable to limit marriage to one woman; when she gets pregnant, the husband becomes like a bachelor or sterile."

"And there are no female slaves nowadays, but men make relationships with lovers and prostitutes, which can be more conducive to waste and trouble."

Napoléon also says: "In France they exaggerate the status of women, although they must not be seen as equal to men, but rather machines to produce children."

"And they [women] revolted during the revolution and formed groups and were made to join the army."

"And they must have been stopped because the society would be prone to trouble and chaos if women stop relying on men. The society is indeed risking significant, unstoppable division."

"And one of the two genders must submit to the other; and once a war is launched between the two genders, it will not be like the war between the rich and poor or between the black and white."

"There is no doubt that divorce is harmful to women. For the man who marries several women together does not appear to have issues, unlike the woman who marries several men; she deteriorates significantly."

This is how Napoléon admitted the necessity of marriage in the modern time. How did Linen [Russia] admit this in the big revolution that followed the French revolution? He solved the marriage problem by dissolving the tie of marriage itself. For [to him] the marriage tie is not as strong as that between lovers in a hotel or on a road. And there is nothing stranger than making marriage an angelical law than making it like an animal act.

WIVES PUNISHMENT

Before we conclude this chapter about the marital life of the Prophet, let us examine the punishment of wives in Islam and the punishment the Prophet chose. For the punishment of a husband to his wife at the time of anger is a measure of the status he holds for her, as also the way he treats her at good times is a measure of that side. Both conditions reflect the status of women in general as held by a man.

Quran has set rules for punishment in the case of ill-conduct, namely admonition, refusal to share bed, abstinence from intimacy, and beating: "*As to those women on whose part you see ill-conduct, admonish them (first), (next), refuse to share their beds, (and last) beat them (lightly, if it is useful), but if they return to obedience, seek not against them means (of annoyance). Surely, Allah is Ever Most High, Most Great – Quran, 4:34.*" "*And when you have divorced women and they have fulfilled the term of their prescribed period, either take them back on reasonable basis or set them free on reasonable basis. But do not take them back to hurt them, and whoever does that, then he has wronged himself –Quran, 2:231.*"

The Prophet (PBUH) did not divorce any wife he wedded and lived with, and he had never beat any of them. And it was never documented that he had beaten a servant, let alone a wife. On the contrary, what was narrated by his close circle reveals the opposite. For he used to hate and censure beating women, as he said: "Let him feel shame the man who beats his wife as he beats his slave. He beats her during the day and sleeps with her at night!"

For Quran advises that man could resolve to beat his wife for an ill-conduct only as a last resort if everything else has failed. And scholars surrounded this option with conditions that prevent physical harm and limit the action to the minimum that can make this solution successful.

The thing that can be best understood from allowing the option of beating is that some women cannot be straightened, except with this kind of discipline, and these types of women may be known to accept it and do not denounce it. These women may not be necessarily from those psychotics who enjoy this act as some kind of sadism.

Yet the punishment that the Prophet chose is long isolation after initial admonition and gentle blame, not like others who hasten to apply physical punishment.

And isolation, especially in the bed, is a very tough psychological punishment, not a physical one that hurts the woman for what she misses from the sexual activities. For missing on the sexual side for days is not as painful for a woman like isolation, which makes this option of punishment one of the toughest, except when compared with divorce.

In his book: "A Call to the Fair Gender", Mr. Rashid Reda said: "Isolation is a discipline to the woman who loved her husband and suffered from his isolation. And this isolation cannot be achieved by merely not sharing the bedroom as a whole or not sharing the bed; but it can be achieved by abstaining from intimacy, whereas physically leaving the bed or the room is a punishment that was not permitted by Allah, which could be a reason to worsen the conflict. There is an effect in sexual abstinence that may not be achieved by physically leaving the bed or the bedroom, for sharing the same bed is what arouse intimacy that brings tranquility to both partners and settles any roughness. When the husband abstains from the intimacy, he hopes that this act will motivate her to discuss the issue in response to her quest for the missing tranquility and associated feelings, which eventually bring her from the ill-conduct to accord. And I can imagine my reader to concur with this outcome."

But what we [the Author] see is that Mr. Rashid Reda missed the delicate goal behind this psychological punishment [abstinence from intimacy], whereas the actual wisdom is way deeper than what he thought. There is no doubt that the severest punishment is the one that touches a person's pride and shakes his very essence, and makes him/her suspects the very quality that makes him/her feel the person he/she is.

The woman knows that she is weaker than man, but this does not bother her much since she is aware that she fascinates him and that she beats him with her beauty, and she can compensate for her weakness with the desire and yearning he holds for her. So let him [man] be strong as much as he likes, for she possesses beauty and captivation, and her biggest solace for her weakness is that her charm is irresistible, which is sufficient for her to replace the physical strength of body and mind. Therefore, when the woman approaches her husband in her most tempting form, and then he does not succumb, what thoughts will the woman have in this case? Is it the regret of a missed pleasure, or an urge to ask and blame? It is neither! What will happen is that she will doubt her very femininity and she will believe that man when he wills can earn her respect and compliance. And she will appreciate her weakness and does not find solace in her beauty and fascination.

Accordingly, this is a way to discipline the soul not the body, and it is the conflict that completely disarms the woman, since she vainly tried the strongest weapon she possesses but with a defeat that will push her to relinquish arrogance. For she stickles above her weakness when she resorts to her femininity, and once she does and gets disappointed, she will not have something else to stickle with. And here comes the wisdom behind the punishment [of abstinence from intimacy] that cannot be measured by a missing pleasure or seizure of the opportunity to argue and blame.

For the punishment is meant to reverse the rebellion, and nothing can actually reverse a rebellion like when the rebellious appreciates his/her own weakness against the strength of the other party. And abstinence from the intimacy is a means for this call.

Yet the punishment of Prophet Muhammad to his wives is almost non-existent, except that Muslims used to document every small and big thing in his private and public lives. And this fact [absence of punishment] coincides with his long marital life, the many wives he had, the enormous events he had witnessed, and the lack of offspring [from his wives after Khadija] that could have brought ties closer and close cracks [in the marital relationships]. And most of his punishment was akin to the act of a prophet disciplining Muslim women, not his own wives, and in all of his acts of punishment or dutifulness, he was a perfect human in all senses of mercy, wisdom, and fairness.

And when people are not clear about the essence of the Prophet's marital life, there emerges something to manifest about it in that after some 40 years of marriage [i.e. to Lady Khadija], he would still hold this unprecedented purity and faith to that marriage. This is a marital life that is not held by pleasure and intimacy and could never last for that long unless it was founded on love of the hearts, rest of the souls, affection to goodness, and mutual feelings of kindness and respect.

CHAPTER 10: THE FATHER

SPIRITUAL AND BIOLOGICAL FATHERHOOD

CONSERVATION OF SPECIES is one of the greatest secrets in life that has been difficult to fathom and has been troublesome for the greatest scientific and wise minds to explain. It is something that runs consistently through all living things. In this context, we will not try to investigate or explore it here. However, we need to examine some of the observations that can bring us as close as possible to the truth about it.

One of the important observations in this regard is that the concept of conservation of species runs on the premise of reward and compensation in most cases; a shortcoming in one aspect is met with an advantage in another aspect. For example, the primitive and small creatures are vulnerable to broad destruction during birth and growth, but this is counteracted by the production of millions of offspring that guarantee the conservation of the species. On the other hand, bigger creatures produce fewer numbers of offspring requiring prolonged nursing and caring periods, which compensates for the otherwise millions of offspring produced by the small creatures.

Frequent reproduction prevails the case when it is the only way for a member to serve and conserve the species. But once the member of a species finds other ways to serve that species, these other services may take from him [that memebr] the dedication to produce offspring and have his own share of children, as if servicing a species is like a premium imposed on every member of the species but in a variety of forms, so that fulfilling this task in one form exempts that member from all other forms. Or it is like a tax that the talented and gifted member pays back to his own community and species for such [special] bounty.

Humans are the most capable creatures to serve their own species by numerous means that go beyond birth control or reproduction.

In this case, can we say that those great individuals who did not have offspring paid their share in the form of public services, so they do not have to pay their share via reproduction? If we postulate this, then it would just be a rough observation linked to the discussion above. And we do not mean by this observation to achieve any certainty. All we meant from the point we raised above is to give it some consideration in the course of understanding fatherhood.

The fact is that some of the best great individuals who offered astonishing services to mankind did not marry. And the list includes great prophets that no one can doubt their achievements, such as Prophet Jesus (PBUH). In addition, some of these great individuals who married did not produce offspring, or might have had only female offspring, or might have had male and female offspring but they did not survive or live for long due to ill health and body condition.

Biographies of the greats in all aspects of greatness in all nations and eras are full of evidences that reinforce the observation above and render it worthy of review and consideration. This list includes saints, philosophers, scientists, artists, inventors, military generals, and politicians. And it is not difficult for someone to examine any period in a place he is familiar with to find examples of those great individuals and celebrities. There are many examples in Egypt such as Gamaluddin Al-Afghany, Muhammad Abdo, Saad Zaghloul, Abdullah Nadim, Mostafa Kamel, Mostafa Fahmy, Mahmoud Samy Al-Baroudy, and Hafiz Ibrahim.[36]

So, if we allow ourselves to consider the observation above and understand it, and if it is possible for us to realize that serving humankind by offering reforms is in some cases an obligation that can avail someone of the duty of producing offspring, there would not be a context to note it better than in a prophetic mission that addresses a generation after generation and addresses millions in each generation. No fatherhood can compensate for the fatherhood of the flesh and blood, except the fatherhood of a prophet who assumes nurturing souls of his nation, other nations during his time and future nations till the end of time.

We mention this when we recall the share of Muhammad (PBUH) of the spiritual fatherhood and biological fatherhood.

---

[36] Translator: The Author is Egyptian

And we discern some equivalence in these two sides of fatherhood that is worthy of consideration. The price of reforms is certainly a hefty one! Indeed the reformers are the most entitled to reward and exaltation!

For Muhammad, the father, was the best father, and he was grieved by the death of his two sons in a tragedy that warrants the patience of the prophet to cope with the associated pain.

[The fact is that] an individual may not be a good friend, or a good master, or a good husband, but he can still be a good father; dutiful to his children. For the kinship between fathers and children is the closest in terms of emotion, and it is more likely to move the heart of even the toughest individual. How about the fatherhood of someone who was good for friendship, good for mastery, and good for marriage, because his soul provided kindness to the relative and the stranger, and to the weak and strong? This is a father whom we understand how he could rejoice with his children. And we can also know how he would grieve for the loss of those children.

It is likely that fatherhood emotion was at the peak in the Prophet's heart for his son [whole he lost] because he gave him the name of his grandfather [Prophet Ibrahim (Abraham)], hoping that he will succeed him. And it is likely that this fatherly emotion manifested strongly in the way he escorted his little dead boy to his final resting place more than it manifested in his birth.

Many reasons inspired Muhammad (PBUH) to have a strong passion for the long awaited birth of this child. One reason is that Muhammad is an Arab, and he was as keen to have offspring as every man in an Arab clan and alliance would: they prided themselves in ancestry and in offspring. They preserve the history of their ancestors and aspire to have offspring in a way that may not be familiar to others in modern times, although the passion for offspring is an instinct imprinted in every soul.

And Muhammad liked to have children, and he wanted the same for his nation. He recommended that Muslims should increase in numbers as much as they could, so that he can pride himself on their great numbers and status. Therefore, his passion for having male offspring is an Arab nature like it is a human nature and a prophetic nature, which is expected to have a compounded effect for this passion.

However, another reason for the Prophet's strong desire to have male children is the long time that passed after Lady Khadija had given birth to his boys, and the gloating expressed by his rivals in calling him 'the cut off', and this is why Chapter 108 of the Quran was revealed: "The Abundance."

None of the Prophet's wives begot for more than 20 years. And all his children died during this period, except his daughter Fatima, who died six months after him. Al-Qassem and Al-Taher died as babies, whereas Zainab, Roqaiyah, and Umm Kolthum died after they had got married; nothing had offset his grief over the loss of his children, even a little.

These are griefs that increase the passion to a new child, and this is a long time that increases the love to this awaited child. Although we do not know accurately the exact period that his wives spent without giving birth, we can explain some of the reasons behind this for the many circumstances that cannot be necessarily coincidental.

For in relation to his wife Aishah, the Prophet (PBUH) died when she was almost 20 years old, and this is an age the woman can reach without achieving pregnancy, even if she does afterward. But as for the rest of his wives who had marriage before him, we are not aware that they had children before him, except for Ramla Umm Habibia and Hind Bint Ummaya Al-Makhzoumiyah, who were relatively old and at the age where the woman may have lost fertility when the Prophet married them. Accordingly, except for these two women, the rest of the Prophet's wives did not bear children from the Prophet or from anyone else before him. This coincidence is not difficult to explain when we recall the reasons the Prophet had when he married them in the first place, where he offered them the honorable shelter and the kinship connection with his rival clans, but he did not enter the marriage for the sake of offspring. And some of these women, if not most of them, went through tough hardships, fears, and strenuous emigration journeys that could cause sterility in otherwise fertile women. When we add to this the rough living and the premium [or compensative contribution] referred to above that is associated with the greatness of the prophethood plus how the Prophet (PBUH) had been occupied in his 50s to 60s with strengthening the religion and combating the unrest, we can understand the reasons behind this aspect.

FATHERHOOD GRIEF

The passion of the Prophet to have a child lasted for long [after Lady Khadija]. And his anticipation was being renewed every time he had a marriage until the Christian Maria[37] came to him from a far place, and she was not picked on the basis of any of the reasons discussed above [as a shelter for the grieved women or a connect with clans]. Maria gave him the glad tiding, which he hoped to be a boy; this good news invoked his 20 years of passion and an endless hope. And his son Ibrahim finally arrived!

[Ibrahim is] the child that his father looked at when he was born and the hope stretched over hundreds and thousands of years. And he chose for him the name that could have unlimited offspring like the name of his grandfather [Prophet Abraham],

---

[37] Translator: Maria was a Christian slave sent as a gift to the Prophet by the Vicegerent of Egypt, Muqawqis (as called in the Islamic literature).

so that he could be a father and have offspring, generation after generation.

And then died this little boy, and with him died the great hope; they both died when the father was at his 60. What a blow in his twilight years! What hope in life! The religion is now complete, and this kinship has fallen, so there is nothing in life that can be anticipated and prepared for; all of it now is for bridling and ending. The child died before he reached two years of age.

It is a small grief if the pain is measured by the age of the lost ones. But the grief in those we lose is measured by how much we feel and care for them. And the young is in more need of kindness and care than the grown, independent one. It is measured by how much they rely on us, and the reliance of the young on his caregiver is way greater than the reliance of an adult. The grief is also measured by how much hope we hold for the lost ones, and hope is longer at the beginning of the road than in the middle. Moreover, the pain that is associated with losing the beloved ones is measured by the age of those who suffer the loss. And what a greater loss than at the gate into 60 years of age in the only hope that links the present with the past and future.

I have never imagined Muhammad (PBUH) in a situation nearer to the human grief and heartache than when he was standing on the verge of the grave of his little boy, shedding tears, anguished, and supplicating. For this is a soul [Muhammad] that instilled hope in thousands after thousands, and here he is with his own dear hope severed, and unfortunately cannot be revived even by all the hopes that a reformer inspired in the whole life. And I can imagine Muhammad on that day closer to the hearts of the successors more than those sitting around him and closer to his soul.

His wives were the closest to him, and they loved him the best a wife can love her husband, but their love in this situation was not bringing any comfort, because it was the love that brought forth jealously from the mother of the born boy. This veiled part of that love is proportional to the jealousy and the magnitude of the love itself. And, in this, they are not blameworthy, since it is a human's nature that they did not set up and were not able to control.

And his companions were also the closest to him, sitting in humbleness before him; their admiration for him as a prophet made them forgot that he is a father, but rather a father more compassionate than any other father. They thought that the Prophet does not grieve like some people believe that the brave man does not fear and does not love life, and that the generous man does not appreciate the value of money. But the heart that does not fear is not entitled to the credit of bravery, and the heart that does not grieve is not eligible for the credit of patience. For the virtue is in the grief that one can overcome, and in the fear that one can rise above, and in knowing the value of the money that one can donate.

And the virtue of the Prophet, both in his prophethood and fatherhood, is that he grieved and wept. And this is the connection between him and the human's heart and between him and humans. And where is such Prophet who this connection between him and humans' hearts is disconnected [i.e. none]; such connection that unites scattered hearts?

Usama Ibn Zaid narrated that Zainab, the daughter of the Prophet (PBUH) sent him: "My daughter is dying, if you can come to us." The Prophet replied: "It is all to Allah, whatever he gave and whatever he took, and everything is destined. Observe patience and ask Allah for the reward." She sent back to him, requesting by Allah that he must go to her. The Prophet went to her and held the child while in the last breath. The Prophet shed tears. And Saad asked him: "What is this Oh Messenger of Allah?" He replied: "This is a mercy that Allah instilled in the hearts of whom he wills. And none would show mercy to Allah's slaves, except the merciful ones."

This is the Messenger of Allah in the most truthful moment that glows the message of messengers: in mercy and human relationships. And without these traits, a human can never be a messenger.

And Muhammad avoided seeing his granddaughter dying at his old age. How about his grief for his son Ibrahim, a piece of his flesh, at a time the hope to have offspring has weaned?

The grief of the Prophet over the death of his son was equal to his joy when the boy was born; and his joy in his birth was proportional to the hope he had in him and the passion he had for his coming.

And all of the human kindness concentrated in this righteous soul [Muhammad] during its generosity in rejoicing for his newly born child. The joyful father shaved the hair of his son and paid his weight worth charity in silver to the poor. And this is how far that man went, although he was the most capable and resourceful individual on the planet at the time, including kings and chiefs. He brought on his utmost joy and brought on his utmost bestowal. And had he willed he would have weighed the child worth of jewellery and gems, which would amount to only a little of what he could have offered on that blessed day.

And as much as the joy for his arrival was the grief over his death. The man who carried the burdens of the whole world was unable to carry his own feet!

He left the [graveyard] leaning on a kind friend for the last time he carries his son in his fatherly lap before he buries him in the dust. And he was facing the mountain when he said: "Oh Mountain, if you are through what I am going through you would have collapsed, but we are to Allah, and to him we return."

Indeed by Allah, it is one of the calamities that can be taken by the flesh and blood, but cannot be carried by the rocks of mountains!

He grieved the way he was supposed to mourn. But the grief that he was not meant to have is the one that goes with whooping. And it is what the Prophet denounced when the sun was eclipsed and Muslims thought it was mourning the death of the child, but the father (who the sun indeed eclipsed in his eyes) said: "Nay, the sun and the moon are two signs of Allah. They do not eclipse for the death or life of anyone."

They [sun and moon] actually do [eclipse], but in the heart of the mournful ones not in the heart of the sky!

THE NOBLEST FATHER

It appears that Muhammad was the exemplary father as he was the exemplary Prophet. This is how it was predestined. For we saw in Muhammad the example when his son Ibrahim was born, and we saw in him the example when his son was gone. A child would never wish – if children can wish – fatherhood more compassionate and noble than this fatherhood in both situations.

In fact, Muhammad was rather an exemplary father for any relative, close or far, male or female, and young or old.

Have you seen him when Al-Hassan, the son of his daughter Fatima, entered and rode his back while he was praying? A Prophet in his prayer is in his noblest and most sublime moment. But the Prophet in his sublime and noble manners prolongs his prostration so that he does not spoil the boy's fun until he gets down voluntarily. And one of the companions asked the Prophet: "You have taken long in your prostration!" And he replied: "My son rode my back and I did not wish to hasten him."

Have you seen Fatima [the Prophet's daughter] when she walks through the house in the most similar way her father walks? Have you seen the love that overwhelms his heart when he sees a girl resembling her father in the way he walks and the way he looks? This is Fatima, the daughter who survived all of his boys and girls. He chose her to confide in at the time of his death: "I am leaving this life," and she cries, "And you are the first to join me," and she laughs. In this laughter and cry at the boundaries between life and death is the purest love and compassion between a father and his child. He pleased her in his prophethood and pleased her in his fatherhood. And she laughed at the moment of farewell because it was the time of reunion. Thus, left this world the noblest Prophet and the noblest father.

CHAPTER 11: THE MASTER

THE NATURE OF GOODNESS

WE TALKED IN THE VARIOUS chapters of this book about Muhammad: as a chief, a friend, a husband, and a father, after talking about his genius in the mission, in leading armies, in politics, in management, and in eloquence.

There remains an aspect without which we cannot fully understand the elements of a human soul in how it interacts with other human souls; that is how a person treats the subordinates he controls. In essence, those subordinates do not have protection, except what derives from the master's manners and character; those are the servants and slaves. Treatment of this group reflects the underlying manners in a way that cannot be equally reflected by any other encounter because it draws from the instinct and faith and cannot be invoked by a command or an invitation.

For friendship involves mutual rights between the two friends; if one of them forgets these rights, the other who honors these rights will readily remind him, despite his ability to meet the aversion with a similar one, even in his inner self. On the other hand, chieftaincy [mastery] could entitle the chief to control and force the subordinates to obey. Yet it rarely goes without the concern of possible anger or revolt [by those subordinates], which could be feared slightly or significantly.

People do not find it wondrous when they see a father showing kindness to his children, for this is a nature instilled in every living father, regardless of the magnitude of kindness of the father and whether he deserves the duty of his children. Similarly, a husband has no choice in showing compassion to his wife for the affectionate relationship between them and the status of his relatively weaker wife, a relationship that compensates for strength and leadership.

But as to an owned slave, there is nothing to protect him other than what is in his master's soul in terms of mercy and goodness. And it is an absolute mercy and goodness when the master follows the religion in treating his slaves and servants who do not have any other support in life. However, it suffices to be a real mercy if it is just limited to the divine commandments, but if it goes beyond this to a voluntary goodness that is not imposed by the religion or the culture and not sought by the slave, this is then the mercy in its pinnacle truth, and it is the best indicator of the manners.

By now, the reader has learned that this book is not meant to explain the fundamentals of Islam and detail the quality of Muhammad's call, for this is beyond the scope of the book, plus numerous scholars have already covered it. But what we really meant to cover in these chapters are the psychological motivations that inspired the Prophet in all his acts and dealings, which are undoubtedly in line with the commandments of the religion. Yet there is a difference between the goodness that derives from commandments and the goodness that is naturally instilled in the soul, and this is what we meant to present herein. Therefore, in covering how Muhammad treated his servants and slaves, we do not intend to include the rulings of Islam and commandments of Quran on this matter. Rather, we intend to discuss the advantage of Muhammad over all masters of this field. And such advantage does not exist in those who just settle for the rulings and commandments [of the religion], or those who reach the pinnacle associated with such rulings and commandments.

ISLAM AND SLAVERY

It is useful in the context of this section to refer briefly to the advantage of Islam over other religions on the issue of slavery and enslavement because some people mix between Islam's acknowledgement of slavery on the one hand and its responsibility for past slavery on the other hand, and they associate Prophet Muhammad (PBUH) to this responsibility.

In this context, we must mention first that none of the other religions forbade any form of slavery, whether that associated with wars or slave trades. On the contrary, some of the top magnates in Christianity such as Saint Augustine considered it a fair punishment to those who got enslaved. And some of the church ministers deprived slaves and servants of serving the church in sermons and guidance sessions, to avoid the impurity of those evil group.

It must be mentioned also that slavery was deeply entrenched in the old economic system of the world, and its elimination was close to impossible. The best way to address this issue was to follow a gradual approach, one step at a time, starting by making it difficult and undesirable for people. And this is what Islam did!

Islam started by making all types of slavery unlawful, except for prisoners of war. Islam then made freeing slaves a favorable deed, and called it a favor and pardon an individual would be thanked for: "*And afterward (set them free) as a favor or for ransom – Quran, 47:4.*"

Afterward, Islam allowed a prisoner of war to ransom himself and made his freedom an obligation that relies in most cases on his will if he can.

And the undoubted truth is that what Islam did was the best that slaves ever received from any religion or legislation. And if there was any [useful] introduction to dismantling slavery, it is the introduction of Islam and nothing else, and this was the best that could be done in the old world system. In such system, the number of slaves was almost identical to the number of free people, as cited in some of the statistics in the Greek and Roman civilization.

One of the most prominent thinkers in history, Aristotle, looked into the issue of slavery. He accepted it and made it a natural thing to exist and that it must actually exist. He also considered bondage to be inevitable to certain groups of people who are incapable of taking care of themselves, and cannot survive without a master or a protector.

MUHAMMAD'S TREATMENT OF HIS SLAVES

Had the Prophet just followed his own religion in treating slaves he would have excelled in this field over the most generous individual in his time. Yet it is the absolute fact when we say without the tiniest exaggeration that many children never wish a treatment from their own parents better than the treatment that Muhammad's servants and slaves had enjoyed. And where is such good father who treats his children in a manner kinder than the way the Prophet treated Zaid Ibn Harithah and his son Usama?

Muhammad freed Zaid and considered him qualified to marry one of his close relatives whom he respected and cared and later married her [Zainab Bint Gahsh] and was one of his dearests. So, not only did Muhammad offer him his freedom and made him equal in terms of provision, but he also raised him to the social status that is only warranted to masters. And nothing can confirm this status as much as the honor associated with marriage. And the Prophet afterward kept this fatherly duty toward his son Usama and privileged him to lead the Shaam army when he was still under 20, despite the fact that the army at the time included some of the most senior companions of the Prophet. Had the Prophet had a son at his age, he would not have cared for him in a better manner or given him a better privilege.

Indeed, we did not deviate from the fact or exaggerated the interpretation when we said that a son would not wish for a better treatment than what Muhammad offered to his slaves. For Zaid knew that Muhammad was better than his father and staying with him was better than getting united to his own family. So he chose to stay with Muhammad over going back with his father. Yet Zaid did not stay with Muhammad and preferred him over his whole family for the sake of the prophethood, as Muhammad was not a prophet at the time. Rather, Zaid stayed with him because Muhammad (PBUH) was the human who even a slave like Zaid knew that his human ties are stronger than the fatherly tie of others.

The love of a father for his child is a legacy of thousands of thousands of generations; it is actually the legacy of love in all living beings. And when the duty toward the disadvantaged people reaches the level of the parental love, it [that duty] has then reached the summit that a climber cannot go beyond.

The Islamic Sharia'a gave the good-doer the option to free the prisoners of war by way of favor, by taking ransom, or through exchange of prisoners. And in all cases, any of these options is a good deed. But for Muhammad, it was the choice of favor and beyond. He set free every prisoner that came his way, and supplemented the freedom with every parental compassion that included all his acquaintances. And he did not allow in his anger what an educator or a father allows for himself in terms of punching and disciplining. And his words to a disobedient servant were closer to leniency than to punishment. An example to this effect is the story of the female slave he sent for something and came late; all he said when she returned: "If not for fearing of the Qisas [requital in punishment], I would have punished you with this Sewak [toothbrush]."

Hitting your child with the toothbrush is not a big deal, but Muhammad fears requital if he uses it in disciplining a slave that disobeyed him, and he is the one that chief of masters obey him!

Anas narrated that the Prophet sent him for an issue, but he strayed toward some children playing in the market, only to find the Prophet grabbing his clothes from behind while laughing: "Oh Onais [nickname of Anas], go to where I asked you!" It is a word that he does not say to his servant, except while calling him with laughter, as if he is blaming his peer. And even a peer may be blamed in a much tougher way!

The Prophet's mercy toward the slaves of others was akin to his mercy toward his own slaves. And he used to compliment them, lift their morale, accept their presents and reciprocate, accept their invitation on food, and advise others to care for them: "They are your brethren and slaves that Allah made you responsible for. So whoever Allah makes responsible for anyone of these brethren, he should feed him from what he feeds, and clothes him from what he clothes himself; do not burden them beyond their ability, and help them in their work."

GOODNESS BY ACTION

Goodness by action in this context is probably nobler and more anti-humiliating compared with mere direct duty to a servant. For direct duty to a servant is kindness to him, but duty via action [helping the servant in doing his job] is a lift of the servant to the status of his master when the latter does not abstain [haughtily] from serving himself by his own hands, and this is what we meant by goodness by action. And this was the norm of the Prophet in his house, family, and servants.

The Prophet used to milk his goat, fix his shoes, serve himself, and feed his she-camel. So when the servants are made to realize that their work is similar to that undertaken by their master who has control over them, this is indeed the equality that negates the feeling of servitude and fixes its repercussion, in a way that is not just limited to direct kindness.

The Prophet (PBUH) did not accept to be served by a servant in cases the free individuals would wish to serve him gratefully. Many men of the highest rank among Muslims actually wished to serve the Prophet in something his servants and slaves volunteered to accomplish. And this is another level of the quality of 'goodness by action' and applying equality between the position of a servant and disciple. For the Prophet, the work of a servant was like a student sitting before his teacher lovingly not submissively, with self-ordained politeness rather than discipline by the tradition and culture.

And thus, the Prophet (PBUH) disliked having his hands kissed fearing this could become habitual among people, which could bring about humiliation and submissiveness. Abu Huraira narrated: "I entered the market with the Prophet (PBUH) and he bought some pants saying to the seller: "Weigh in justice," and the seller jumped on the hand of the Prophet to kiss it, but the Prophet pulled his hand, saying: "This is what the non-Arab do with their kings, and I am not a king, but I am rather one of you," and he picked the pants. I wanted to carry them, but he said: "A person should carry his own stuff."

It is correct to say that the Prophet's share in serving himself was bigger than the share taken by his servants, and that he made the servitude a kind of distributing the tasks or creating a cooperative atmosphere among people in the same house in what each person can contribute: "I am but a slave [to Allah], I eat like a slave and sit like a slave."

This is the word of a master by his leadership, the master by his decent, the master by his authority, the master by attracting hearts around him, and the master by his control over his inner self, his publicity, his opinion, and his desires. And had this mastery prevailed, slavery would have been dismantled, leading to an environment where the differences among ranks would be, like differences among ages, associated with no inferiority toward the disadvantaged or pride of the affluent individuals. It is rather a distribution of business, cooperation among brethren, even if they are not on the equal keel of ranks.

CHAPTER 12: THE WORSHIPPER

THE FOUR NATURAL TRAITS

THE FOUR NATURAL TRAITS that exist at differing strengths among humans are: worship, thinking, beautiful expression, and action and mobility. These four qualities are rarely present in one individual with equal strength. And if they exist concurrently in one person, normally the magnitude of one of them exceeds the others.

The trait of worship calls us to connect with the secrets of the universe for harmony and unification. It calls us to unite with the whole universe into a one big family.

The trait of thinking drives our faculties to explore and discover. It invites us to unite with the universe into one vast laboratory.

The trait of beautiful expression ignites the sacred fire in our inner selves and melts the minerals of beauty into beautiful molds made by our minds and tongues, or made by our minds and hands, or made by our minds and our limbs. It invites us to unite with the universe into a vast museum.

The trait of action and mobility teaches us how to respond to the forces of the universe. They attract us and impart the power that we use to attract them to us. It invites us to unite with the universe into a square of contention and a course of race.

But you rarely feel the universe as being a house for a family, a laboratory for a researcher, an art museum, and a race course simultaneously. It is rather a mutually exclusive single state. The remaining states may follow marginally as an assistant to the main state.

Muhammad, the son of Abdullah, had all of these four traits simultaneously, all in a conspicuous manner. He was a worshipper, a thinker, an eloquent speaker, and a worker who changed the whole life by his own actions. But, he was (PBUH) a worshipper before being anything else. And for this worship, he holistically directed his thoughts, words, actions, and every other trait. He was readied for the role of a worshipper by his legacy, upbringing, and make. He was in the pious house that was serving the Kaaba, and his ancestors were faithful and sincere believers.

And he was raised as an orphan, who lived reclusively, avoided servility lightness and habituated himself to contemplation and observation of his surroundings in a critical manner, with a soul that rose above lowliness and inclined toward purity and straightness of the conscience. And he was physically formed to be a worshipper from his early youth.

It is said that when he was only 2 or 3-years old, he went through a state that historians find it difficult to explain[38]. And those who

---

[38] Translator: It is narrated that the Angles cut open the Prophet's chest and washed his heart with a heavenly fluid before making it good again.

heard it narrated it with some variations, and we do not know which is the most authentic. And some of the European historians rushed to attribute it to some type of epilepsy, without a proven scientific evidence.

All we can emphatically say about this or other incidences is that Muhammad was formed to receive divine revelation and that this formation had some symptoms that must have been noticed since his early age. Because the physical preparation will not take place in a few days, months or years. And this physical preparation must have started when he was still a drop within his father, let alone in his babyhood or early age. It is narrated that when the Prophet was receiving the revelation, he would drop his head, become distressed with his face looking pale and exhausted to the extent that the sweat drops successively from his face in winter with bee-like sounds heard close to his face. It is also narrated that he would get a headache that requires henna around his head [to alleviate the pain]. When his hair turned grey, he said, "Houd and its sisters [Chapters from Quran] turned my hair grey." And he counted other chapters from the Noble Quran when he was asked about its sisters.

This is not the default formation of every human being, but the formation that receives revelation, comprehends a secret, and gets shaken by serious news.

THE WORSHIPPER'S TRAIT

And his traits in the absence of revelation were in harmony with his capacity to receive the revelation and prophethood, for he was all feelings and all life. When someone sees him, he sees a vigilant heart that picks on every spiritual move and every subtle indicator. When he walks, he would walk briskly with a forward-leaning gait; when he turns, he would do with his whole body; when he points, he would point with all of his hand; when he thinks, he would lower his gaze or raise it toward heaven; when he supplicates, he would raise his hands until his armpits are visible; when he gets angry, his eyes and cheeks get red; his sweat fills his forefront; and he sleeps with his heart awake. He enjoyed a sensitive conscience that contemplated the unseen and awakened his inner self to the subtlest matter and made him always in a state ready to receive the revelation.

This is the attribute of a worshipper who thinks, expresses and acts, and not the attribute of a worshipper who applies himself to only worship or to only think, or does like a hermit who lost his body strength and can only reside in a cell or live in abstinence.

Muhammad's worshipping was a temporary seclusion or admiration of the wonders of the universe which otherwise people find it normal, because they were not gifted in their sights and insights with this new look that sees everything as newly created.

The fascination of the observer who sees that the sun is just being created today before his eyes cannot be matched. And it is the same fascination of the eyes that refuses to get tired from the normality, because it is always looking newly at things or seeing in every scene a new creation.

And thus was the worship of Muhammad (PBUH): fascination by the wonders of the universe in every look as if he sees the usual things for the first time, and contemplation of the creation that drives him toward faith, because faith starts with fascination, with actually endless cycles of fascination and contemplation.

Muhammad is the restorer of faith in humans' hearts. He was renewing his faith the same way he was renewing his wonderment every day. And he used to supplicate: "Oh Controller of the hearts, make my heart steadfast in your religion." And when asked about this, he said: "There is no human being but his heart is between two fingers of Allah's; he makes steadfast or send astray whomever he wills." This is a mental agility that is always evolving in awareness, contemplation, and conscience: no entire dedication to the awareness at the expense of worshipping, and no entire dedication to worshipping at the expense of the awareness. Rather, it is the contemplation of someone who will act upon, not the contemplation of someone who abandon the action to dwell into postulations, probabilities, and doubts. One-third of his time was dedicated to his lord, one-third to his family and one-third to himself. Yet his time for himself or his family never detached him from worshipping and connecting with his lord.

He was fascinated by beauty from a young age: the beauty of the sun, the moon, the day, the night, the desert, the gardens, and the beauty of human faces that he saw through the goodness he was seeking. He was contemplating the goodness in the beauty. It is the beauty of Allah that was calling upon him every time he saw something beautiful. He thought of the creation to believe in the creator, and then settled there in tranquility. He said: "Satan will come to one of you asking: who created heaven? He [Satan] says, Allah. Who created the earth? He [Satan] says Allah. He [Satan] then asks: who created Allah? Anyone among you experiences this should say: I believe in Allah and his Messenger."

This is the last stop of the contemplation of a sound mind that was created to act and teach people to worship and act. It was not created to be consumed in postulations and suffer from doubts.

And with this, we ask: how far did the thinkers that dwelled in their doubts and got swept by the extremity of their assumptions reach? How far did Kant (the top thinker of our modern time in this area, if not of all times) reach? He concluded that the being is two beings: inner being and real being; and the world is two worlds: a perceived world and real world. The real being realizes the real world when in its pure form, and does not go beyond this toward the phenomenal world associated with expressions and words.

Interpretation of the above idea means that the faith of the inner being is independent of proofs and evidences. And that the ultimate reference is the faith and nothing but the faith. And let us read what he said about the grand evidence on God's existence.

He says: "The nonexistence is non-existent. Therefore the world is existing. And if you believe in the world, you must believe in its perfect form, because you need justification to assume any imperfection, whereas you do not need a justification to assume the perfection in a world that does not encounter nonexistence."

But what is the difference between believing in God and believing in the world in its perfect form? Here exaggerating the assumptions and doubts reach its peak. And here the faith peaks without exaggerating the assumptions and doubts. Cannot the two ends meet? Is it not a fact that the assumptions and doubts can get wrong? And in this case, the whole matter reduces to a mere belief.

For this reason, the Prophet frequently advised in his spiritual worshipping to always think of Allah's creation and avoid thinking of his being [form]: "Think of Allah's bounties but do not think of him, least you perish." And in a holy saying: "I was hidden treasure and I then wanted to be known; so I created the people and became known," or in another narration: "So I created people, so they knew me by me."[39]

THE ROAD TO THE DESTINATION

The essence of the prophetic sayings above, and others, is that thinking of the facts of the world and the universe is the road to know Allah, and there is no other way of using faculties, mind or instinct to achieve this: belief in the eternal existence in its perfect being and pondering at the facts in this world as we see it, feel it, and understand it. And this is the best a faith can do, and the best philosophy could offer, and the best science can provide, considering the limitations of science. And this is the knowledge that the Prophet made compulsory on every male and female Muslim. Ibn Abbas narrated that the Prophet said: "It is [the knowledge] better than praying, fasting, performing pilgrimage and fighting in Allah's cause," because this is [through knowledge] the way to know Allah.

We find it mandatory, after mentioning all of the above, that Muhammad is a prophet, and the Prophet teaches all people faith. And this is the way for all people in what is made available to them in terms of pondering and thinking. For people can get lost in the errors of doubts and contradictions laid by philosophers and logicians. And people cannot arrive at any

[39] Translator: This Hadith Qudsy (Holy saying) has been falsified by Muslim Scholars. (e.g. http://fatwa.islamweb.net/fatwa/index.php?page=showfatwa&Option=FatwaId&Id=14995)

guidance better and more secure than believing in the creator and pondering at his creation. It is either guidance or sterile error. And it is not for a prophet to block the road to guidance and open the road to deviation.

We have talked in this Chapter about the spirit of worship or the natural trait that inspires the worshipper into his spiritual worship.

And as for the explicit rituals, this is the ritual of Islam as ordained on all Muslims. The Prophet prayed, observed fasting, performed pilgrimage, and paid alms in accordance with the Sharia'a that Muslims follow. And the Prophet used to ask of himself what he did not ask of others, in a manner that reflects both tolerance and ease, a feature known in his deeds and traits.

For he used to be the softest [quickest] when he leads people in prayers, and the longest when he prays by himself. And he may stand up most or part of the night, but never asked others to pray or fast like him. On the contrary, he advised others to worship in moderation and not to be hard on themselves, otherwise they would be like the Munbatt[40]: "Neither did he progress in his journey nor did he keep his ride alive." For people receive worship orders in the form of mandatory obligations. But the prayer for the soul that is accustomed to worship is a monologue

40 Translator: the Munbatt is the one who goes harshly on his camel during a journey in the desert until it dies in the middle of the road.

of love and joy of standing before God and compliance with the propensity of the heart and faculties, equally.

And Muhammad used to: “Resort to prayers when he encounters a difficulty.” And this is how when the soul goes through a difficulty it reverts to whom it loves to reduce the burden, relieve the distress, feel the company after estrangement, and find the guidance after confusion.

And once the soul feels the joy of standing before God in prayers, there will be no physical strain, or distress. Rather, there will be a relief from the tiredness and a reprieve from distress, especially if the soul possesses the capacity to spend that much of the night and the day in worshiping and still accomplishes its duties and thinks laterally, and no one around could suspect that there is ever any negligence to any of the rights of that soul or the rights of other humans by applying oneself to worshipping during the night or the day.

CHAPTER 13: THE MAN

THE CHOSEN

THERE LIVED IN THE PAST many of the great individuals whose traits were documented through hearing or in pictures and monuments. Yet the life of none of these great individuals was fully and accurately preserved as the life of Prophet Muhammad (PBUH) was documented by his companions and those who were coeval with him. For we know him by description better than we know some of the immortalized individuals by their informative pictures and monuments. Because pictures and statues may tell the facial features and external attributes, and may also enable the insightful to infer some of the subtle qualities. Yet they [the pictures and statues] do not describe them to us in any detail as much as the biography of the Prophet was preserved in every state he had been through, in every gesture, in his look and appearance, in the way he ate and drank, in the way he prayed and fasted, in his staying or travel, and in his silence and talking. Because those who described him loved him, loved to follow his example, and wanted to be accurate in describing him. And in following this accuracy, they invoked all means of salvation and conservatism. Accordingly, the responsibility that was associated with describing the Prophet was a mix of worshipping and kindness and an act of following the [prophetic] traditions and accomplishing duties. [In this regard, it is noted that] the description of the Prophet was [consistent and] never varied, except like when someone looks at the same face every now and then and describes it differently every time, albeit without revealing any kind of contradiction or intention of twisting the reality.

The summary of the preserved narrations is that the Prophet (PBUH) was a rare example of the beauty of Arabian manhood. He was perfect in this aspect from all angles, like in his all other traits. For a man may be handsome, but unlikeable. And a man may be handsome, likeable, but unrespectable. And a man may be handsome, likeable, and respectable, but he does not like people, unkind to them and does not exchange loyalty and friendship.

But Muhammad (PBUH) was perfect in his handsomeness, affection, respect, and kindness to people. And thus he was of the traits that his descriptors and loving ones can ever wish, and he was indeed worthy to be named the 'chosen.'

[In terms of the physical description], when someone sees the Prophet, he would see a man with a rosy tinge, wide forehead, prominent head, wavy hair, closely-knit eyebrows with a vein in between that would bulge upon anger, large and black eyes with long black eyelashes, high nose, smooth cheeks, wide mouth, thick beard, long beautiful neck, broad shoulders, long wrists, large fleshy hands, somewhat high arches of the feet, slightly above average height that makes him neither overly tall nor short and well-proportioned with a strong physique, neither overweight nor slim.

When he moves, the observer would see a man of vitality. He walks as if walking downhill. When he raises his leg, he raises it all as if all his bode expands; when he turns, he turns with the whole of his body; when he points, he points with all of his hand; when he talks, he brings his left hand toward his right hand and strikes with his right thumb on his left-hand palm; when he speaks, he speaks clearly with his jaws during opening and closing; and he may bite his lip when he talks. And despite his vitality, he was shyer than a virgin, with a radiant face. When he dislikes something, it can be seen on his face, and when he approves something, it can also be recognized in his smiley look.

The vitality and shyness of the Prophet were associated with power and determination in this beautiful physique. He did knock down the strong man, rode the horse without utilities and domesticated it, and teased his beloved wife to race him. Lady Aishah said: “I went with the Prophet (PBUH) in one of his trips when I was still young and slim, and he asked his people to move forward and they did. He then said to me: “Let us race” and we ran and I was able to beat him. He said nothing. In another journey, when I gained weight, he asked his people to move forward, and asked me to race him, and he won me. He laughed and said: “One against one.””

This race took place when he was close to 60, which indicates juvenility of his soul plus the juvenility of his limbs.

This liberality was manifest in his relationship with everyone in his family or companions. He acclimated and softened his seriousness to turn into compassion toward every grieved, mercy toward every weak, and adjusted to all emotions.

Anas Ibn Malek narrated: "The Prophet (PBUH) entered my mother's house and found my brother Abu Umair sad. He asked: "Oh Umm Salim, why is Abu Umair sad?" She said: "His little bird that he used to play with has died." The Prophet said to him: "Abu Umair, what happened to the bird [in a rhymed manner]?" And he kept asking him every time he saw him. This is a little story full of kindness and cheerfulness from any angle one may consider. For the master [the Prophet] visits his servant [Anas] in his house, and asks his mother about the sadness of his brother, and offers him solaces, and keeps remembering him afterward.

Another example of his nature in this regard is his appreciation of human weakness in someone like Abdullah Al-Khammar [the wine drinker], who was known for his drunkenness and sense of humor. The Prophet applied the punishment of drinking wine to him, while still laughing at his jokes [in other occasions].

APPROVAL OF HUMOR

Nuaiman Ibn Amro was the most famous among the Helpers [Al-Ansaar] for his sense of humor, and he did not spare anyone of his jokes. The Prophet used to smile every time he sees him. And in a few occasions, he joked with the Prophet for what he knew about his tolerance and approval of humor. A Bedouin came to the Messenger of Allah, entered the mosque, and made his camel to kneel down in the yard outside. Some of the companions whispered to Nuaiman: "If you can slaughter the camel for us to eat, for we are craving meat; and the Prophet should pay for it" And Nuaiman did. When the Bedouin left the mosque and saw his camel dead, he cried: "Oh Muhammad, my camel has been killed!" The Prophet went out and asked: "Who did this?" They said: "Nuaiman." The Prophet tracked him until he found him at the house of Dubaah Bent Al-Zubayr Ibn Abdulmotalib hiding in a hole and covered with palm leaf stalk. And a man pointed to him with his finger shouting: "I did not see him Oh Messenger of Allah." And the Prophet got Nuaiman out of the hole with his face full of dust, and said: "Why did you do what you did?" Nuaiman said: "Those who mentioned me to you Prophet of Allah." The Prophet kept wiping the dust of Nuaiman's face while laughing and paid for the camel.

And this Nuaiman is the one who sold an employee of Abu Bakr, knowing that the Prophet will definitely know of his act. Abu Bakr travelled to Bosra for trading and took two of his employees with him: Nuaiman and Swait Ibn Harmala. Nuaiman approached Swait and asked him for food, but the latter refused until Abu Bakr comes back. Nuaiman swore that he would upset him. He sent to some people and said: "Would you buy my slave?" And they said: "Sure." He said: "This slave is talkative and he will tell you that he is not my slave and that he is a free man. Would you then abandon the deal if he says so?" They say: "Nay. We will buy him and pay 10 camels." Nuaiman brought the man over to them, and they arrested him and put his hat over his neck. Swait kept saying that he is a free man, etc. But they ignored him and said: "Stop these tricks that we knew already." When Abu Bakr came back and asked about him, Nuaiman told him the story. And they both went to save Swait after paying the ransom. When they told the Prophet on their way back, he laughed and kept laughing for a year every time he saw Nuaiman.

It is the vastness of the soul that enables a man to undertake the noblest, most serious, and respectful missions such as establishing faith, reforming a nation, and changing the course of history, but still happily accommodates humor and offers kindness to those funny individuals and engages in their fun casually. For earnestness is associated with a strictness that can consume soul and make it non-accommodative of this gentle side of life. Yet souls would not get consumed so earnestly unless for some narrowness in the soul and lack in traits, regardless of the accomplishments that could be achieved.

And Muhammad used to accept and make jokes and fun, and his style in this was typical of his style in all his other traits: he gives justice to each trait without affecting any other trait. So he would sincerely joke but never at the expense of honesty and chivalry. For example, Abdulla Al-Khammar [the wine drinker], was receiving from the Prophet the kindness of the big heart despite his weakness in submitting to wine. But, simultaneously, he was receiving from the Prophet the penalty that does not violate the religion or compromise the Sharia'a. It is the kindness that suits the Prophet in the best way, because it suits man in its best form.

So in his humor, Muhammad used to give justice to joy and cheerfulness, without taking from the right of truthfulness and honor. His humor was then a sign of prophethood as much as it was a sign of being a human. And it was never an extraordinary contradiction in a noble Prophet.

The Prophet said to his aunt Safiyah: "No old woman will enter paradise." She cried! He said, while laughing: "Allah glory be to him," he continued: "*Indeed, We have produced the women of Paradise in a [new] creation. And made them virgins. Devoted [to their husbands] and of equal age - Quran, 56:35-37.*"" She understood the point and regained her satisfaction and hope.

A man asked the Prophet for a camel. The Prophet promised to give him a child of a she-camel. The man said: "Oh Prophet what can I do with a child of a she-camel?" The Prophet said: "A camel is not but a child of a she-camel!"

And he said to his nurse Umm Ayman in her old age: "Cover your face Umm Ayman." On another occasion, he heard her on the day of the Battle of Hunayan calling upon Muslims [not to flee] in her non-Arabic accent: "Sabatta Allaho Aqdamakom [wrongly saying May Allah chop off your heads instead of saying May Allah support you]." The battle did not distract him from listening to her amid the war and sword dangers, saying to her: "Do not say that Umm Ayman, for you twist the words." This gentle humor in this feared time was like a soft pat from the master of eloquence to this innocent accent.

MUHAMMAD'S GENEROUS SOUL

This bountiful generosity of Muhammad is the inner beauty that perfected Muhammad's external beauty in People's eyes. And this is Muhammad's repay to the love and respect they had for him in their hearts. Or it is the tie that connects his heart to their hearts within the domain of the human family: they loved him and he loved them; they felt for him and he felt for them. And the issue is not that he was merely a handsome, beloved, and respected person. Rather, it is a handsomeness that encountered the eyes with beauty, and it was a generosity and vastness of the soul that responded to other souls with beauty.

And this generosity of the soul was well entrenched in his inner self to the extent that it seeped voluntarily and naturally in all of his traits and relationships with people, especially the weak and disheartened. For he was the keenest person to settle broken hearts, treat souls, offer solaces, refrain from insult, follow on and visit his companions young and old, respect those of high ranks and the general public to the extent that the humblest thinks there is no dearest to the Prophet than him, sit in any available spot when he joins a group, listen to everyone without interruption (even for a long time), stay patiently when someone sits with him until the person voluntarily leaves, and keep his hand when someone picks it until he releases.

It was his tradition to accept invitations and advise others to do the same. And he never rejected the invitation of a slave, servant, or a female slave or a poor person. And with regards to his recommendations in relation to etiquettes of parties and food gatherings: "If you get invited by two people at the same time, answer the one next to your door for the merit of neighborhood's right, but answer whoever presents the invitation first."

He used to offer greetings first to whomever he encounters. And greet children with peace when he sees them, and he would lighten his prayers if someone comes asking him something.

He used to avoid anger as much as possible, treating it spiritually by praying and supplicating, or treating it physically by sitting if he was standing, or reclining if he was sitting and refusing to move while he is angry.

HIS SOCIAL MANNERS

In his social manners, Muhammad was an exemplary for courteous men in every era. For example, he was never seen stretching his leg before his companions. He used to ask for his host's permission when he leaves after a visit. He never blew in his food or drink, or breath in a container. And when he sneezes he would cover his mouth with his hand or clothes. And when he wakes up at night, he would clean his teeth with the Meswak [special toothbrush]. And he was using this Meswak habitually and advised Muslims to use it after food and in the morning. He used to wear perfume and was very vigilant about cleanness and hygiene, advising his companions: "Shower on Friday, even if you pay one dinar for a cup of water."

Social habits may differ among generations in small issues that have no impact on good manners and sensibility; as people may use fingers or knives and forks to eat; some may wear white clothes while some others wear black, etc. And these are all casual matters that reflect the habits of the time not civility of the character. And there is no problem when people differ in their traditions according to their time from generation to a generation and a nation to another nation. Yet the problem is in what breaches the sound character and courtesy. And these are the two traits in which the Prophet (PBUH) was a model for every courteous man in every time and place. For he never wronged anyone [insulted or did injustice], even slightly; and no one ever complained in his gathering from lack of equitability. And this is indeed the perfect courtesy in its finest meaning.

The person who possesses these traits is a messenger, and the person who possesses these manners is a messenger.

And the essence of his character and manners is that it is leniency in the sights and leniency in the hearts [of others]. For leniency is the one word that sums up all these traits combined. And it is this leniency that elevated Muhammad to the pinnacle of perfection.

And who is the messenger if we were to define some of his features? He is the one who has a self-deterrence toward [wronging] others, young and old, in all dealings with people. Because the first goal of a messenger is to help people establish such deterrent that advises them to embrace goodness and forbids them from the evil and establishes the boundaries to keep. And whoever embraces this as his first mission, his first trait – or his best trait – is to be self-deterrent with self-accountability and questioning. This is the general feature that seeps into Muhammad's manners, blended with all his sayings and deeds. For no one ever questioned Muhammad as much as he questioned himself in guarding the right of the young and old and respecting the safeguard of the capable and incapable individuals.

This is a proof of prophethood that cannot be matched by any other proof, and it is the most worthy of approval. Because it is a proof from the inner self and not an external proof that may be present or absent.

When people have the right criterion to judge Muhammad, they would grant him the highest rank of love and respect. This rank will be granted to him by those who embrace Islam and those who do not, whether religious or not. For humans would never strive to achieve manners and attributes better than those that Muhammad possessed, practiced, and exemplified.

HIS WILL IN FAITH AND ASCETICISM

The person who is most entitled to love and respect is the one who seeks people's prosperity while abstaining from the pleasure of what he controls. For it was proven that Muhammad did not enjoy his life and never ate to fullness for 3 days until he died. Aishah said: "I used to weep for seeing him suffering and rub his stomach to alleviate his feel of hunger, saying: "I protect you by myself, if you can take from life a bit" And he says: "I have no business with this life Aishah! My Brethren Prophets suffered more than this and were patients."""

And Umm Salama described what she found in his house on their wedding night: "A small jar with a bit of barely, a mill, pot, and small cup. I took the barley and ground it and squeezed it into the cup." And this was the dinner of the Prophet (PBUH) and his wife for that night.

Umar saw the marks left on the Prophet's body by the straw mat he slept on and said: "Oh Messenger of Allah! The sand of this straw mat left marks on your body, while the Persians and Romans enjoy the pleasure of this life and they do not worship Allah." The Prophet sat straight and said: "Are you doubting son of Al-Khattab? Those people were given their share of enjoyment early in this life."

He died with his armor mortgaged, with nothing left to his family to inherit. And the humble estate he left behind was not given to his family.

What can anyone say after this about the value of this man, whether he believes in him or not? He may say that he was a prophet who knew that he was a prophet and obeyed and bore the burdens of his mission in obedience and for the sake of making good his creation. This is, in fact, the status and degree of the prophets that Allah chose for them.

On the other hand, if someone denying prophethood altogether were to comment on him, he would say: He [the Prophet] is a good man who wanted goodness to people and he did not know that he was a prophet or that Allah ordered him to convey the message to his creation, but he wittingly rushed to their guidance for no return or reward because he cannot bear any evil coming their way, and at the same time he does not anticipate a return from this life or the hereafter. Whoever says this and belittles the value of a man who loved people that much and cared about their guidance that much is a person who has a distorted conscience.

For Muhammad tops all men: in his formation, in his intention, in his deeds, and in comparison with others who share with him similar mission.

And we can certainly see that Muhammad did not deprive himself [of the pleasures of this life] that much, except to elevate in faith, and to sharpen his will for the sake of this faith and to exhaust his means before Allah and before people in his dedication toward reform.

Muhammad did not dislike the pleasure of his life and did not advise others to hate it or forsake it. So when he contents himself with the limitations he imposed on himself, it is for uplifting his faith based on personal conviction rather than on external influences. It is as if he was concerned that if he receives his share of the life's pleasure, it would be counted as one of the reasons he considered when he delivered guidance to people. Let faith then be the sole goal and all goals, the sole deed and all deeds, and the sole reward and all rewards. And this is what brings comfort to his conscience, and behind this comfort is what people gain from his full efforts in guiding them, undiminished and unsuspected.

If he provides guidance but enjoys life, he would be concerned that this pleasure may be one of his goals. But if he just provides guidance, this guidance is all his hopes and the pinnacle of his hopes. Let him then take from his share of life to compliment his share and the share of his nation of faith. And let this settle his account with himself, his account with his lord, and his account with people.

So what is the essence for all of this? It is the essence of a man who deters himself in secrecy and public, although he is the most deserving to be the deterrent to others. A man no one is like unto him!

CHAPTER 14: MUHAMMAD IN HISTORY

CONNECTION OF HISTORY WITH MUHAMMAD

WE MEANT IN THE PRECEDING chapters to describe Muhammad in his genius, or Muhammad in himself, or Muhammad in his qualities and attributes that are honored equally by those who believe and those who do not believe in him.

And in this final chapter, we wish to briefly discuss Muhammad in history, or Muhammad in the world and grand events. And brevity in this regard should suffice since the world is full of pages that show the position of Muhammad [in the world].

Muhammad himself is great and superbly great, fulfilling every criterion of greatness adopted by humans in all civilization ages. So, what is the position of this greatness in history? Where does it fit in the world and its events, generation after generation?

Its position in history: all the history after Muhammad is connected to him and hooked to his achievements. For there is no one single event that could have ever occurred in the world the way it did if not for Muhammad's appearance and accomplishments!

If not for that orphan who was born in the Arab peninsula in year 571, there would be no conquests in the east or west, no

European movements in the middle age, no crusades, no scientific revolution after these wars, no discovery of the American continent, no conflicts among the Europeans, the Asians and the Africans, no French revolution and the following ones, no World War I or World War II, and no national or international event. The history was something and became something else. In between, there was a new-born starting his life by crying like all other newborns entering the planet.

FAITH CONQUESTS

Yet we judge the greatness of events of the human history based on the conquest of souls rather than conquest of lands. For it is possible that a major event like an earthquake or a flood may cause major, transformational events and conquests that change the face of history and motivate nations. However, what is not possible is to open new horizons and access the worlds of conscience without spiritual greatness inculcated by faith, or without the inner messages that precede these magnificent events.

Islam conquered vast lands because it unraveled in the heart of each of its followers a closed world surrounded by layers of darkness. And Islam did not add to the land that it conquered, for the land does not increase by a new conqueror or by adding a new piece of land, but Islam it actually added to man the best enhancement he could ever achieve, whereby he rises above living animals, and brought him a step closer to the lord. Every conscious person will embrace this fact. On the other hand, he denies this every person who denies the progress of man on the road to the lord.

A European scholar held a comparison between Muhammad, Buddha, and Christ, and asked: "Is not Muhammad somehow a prophet?" And then answered: "He definitely has two of the prophets' virtues: for he knew the truth of God more than those around him and he was overwhelmed by an inner urge to proclaim this truth, and in this he deserves to match the most courageous among the prophets of the children of Israel. Because he risked his own life for the truth, and persevered against the daily abuse for years and forbore the deportation, deprivation, hatred, and friendship. And in all of this, he exercised the utmost patience a person can observe, except for the threat of death that he escaped by the emigration. And despite all of that, he persevered persistently in delivering his message, against the odds of all the spent promises, threats, and temptations to derail him. And it is quite possible that someone from the polytheists reverted to monotheism. But none in the whole world was able to install like Muhammad did a religion based on monotheism that is permanent and stable. And this was never possible except through his powerful determination in persuading others to embrace that call. And if someone asks: "What drove Muhammad to invite others relentlessly to embrace his faith while others [before him] embraced monotheism and kept it to themselves?" There is no escape from admitting that the answer is in the depth and strength of his belief of the truth he is calling for.

The truth that every impartial person, Muslim or Non-Muslim, should consider is this: Muhammad's conquests were conquests of faith; Muhammad's power was a power of faith; and that there is no better description of his achievement than this description and no other justification better than this justification.

The temptations referred to above by the European scholar came to Muhammad when he was calling to his faith while threatened in his very home, and also came to him when he was honored and dignified among those who believed in his call, but he did not pay heed to these temptations, neither when they were out of his reach nor when they were at his discretion.

Utba Ibn Rabeea, the chief of his clan came to him in the beginning of his mission in a gentle and promising mode after Quraysh had failed to sway him by threats: "We have seen no other man of Arabia who has brought so great a calamity to a nation as you have done. You have outraged our Gods and religion and taxed our forefathers and wise men with impiety and error and created strife amongst us. You have left no stone unturned to estrange the relations with us. If you are doing all this with a view to getting wealth, we will join together to give you greater riches than any Qurayshite has possessed. If ambition moves you, we will make you our chief. If you desire kingship, we will readily offer you that. If you are under the power of an evil spirit which seems to haunt and dominate you so that you cannot shake off its yoke, then we shall call in skillful physicians to cure you."

"Have you said it all?" Asked Muhammad (PBUH); and then hearing that all had been said, he spoke forth, and said:

"*In the Name of Allah, the Most Beneficent, the Most Merciful. Hâ-Mîm. [These letters are one of the secrets of the Quran, and none but Allah (Alone) knows their meanings]. A revelation from Allah, the Most Beneficent, the Most Merciful. A Book of which the verses are explained in detail; — a Quran in Arabic for people who know. Giving glad tidings [of Paradise to the one who believes in the Oneness of Allah (i.e. Islamic Monotheism) and fears Allah much (abstains from all kinds of sins and evil deeds.) and loves Allah much (performing all kinds of good deeds which He has ordained)], and warning (of punishment in the Hell-fire to the one who disbelieves in the Oneness of Allah), but most of them turn away, so they listen not. And they say: Our hearts are under coverings (screened) from that to which you invite us – Quran, 41: 1-5.*"

So the Prophet realized the point made by Utba, but neither wealth nor pleasure was in his slightest consideration. Also, the pleasure that was at his discretion [later when Islam prevailed] was not more successful in tempting him than the one that was promised [by Utba]. In fact, the pleasure that was within his discretion was much greater than what Utba Ibn Rabeea'a even dreamt of, but the Prophet's rejection of the available pleasure was even stronger than the one promised. But why all this? Why all the struggle? Why to suffer? And why the patience if not for the faith? And who is that Prophet that would have a status to intercede more than the intercession [for his nation on the day of judgement] of that Prophet and a message greater than this message [of Muhammad]? And what type of person is that who does not appreciate prophets if the prophethood of Muhammad does not earn his appreciation?

History is the judge between Muhammad and his rivals; the judgement of history is more credential than the judgement of either rivals or friends. And it is also more credential than the judgement between the polytheists and monotheists because it is the decree of God. And God decreed that in his acts, Muhammad was in himself an example for the courteous people, and in his acts, Muhammad was the greatest man influencing the world, and in his faith, Muhammad was a believer instilling faith and the man of a religion that lasts as long as the earth exists.

With this, a crescent will appear on the horizon and another will disappear; a moon will appear at night after night; and months will succeed each other. All these [time elements] will write the history of hearts and faculties, because humans do not wait for these [time elements] to document agricultural seasons, business times, or the roles of public offices and governments. But they wait for them [time elements] as guidance in the darkness and tranquility at night, akin to the guide influenced by faith in the darkness of conscience.

THE CAVE DAY

Moons will succeed moons and lunar years will pass one after another, as if heaven provides an indicator pointing to the landmark of a special spot on earth: the emigration cave. Or, they may be pointing to a day for Muhammad that was the best day in his entire life, because it is the day that best marks his mission, most sincere to his call and most hopeful to his soul; and it is the day that Muslims chose for their calendar by inspiration superior to education or investigation.

Why does the day of emigration mark the history of Islam? Why was not the Islamic calendar inspired by the day of the Battle of Badr, Prophet's birthday or the farewell pilgrimage of the Prophet? Each of these [other] days could have been, at a first glance and first thought, worthier to be both the mark of the Islamic calendar and honor than the day that is associated with an escape to save the life [of Muhammad] and faith in the middle of the night. For the man [Umar] who chose the emigration day to mark the beginning of the Islamic calendar was wiser and more knowledgeable about faith, belief, and everlasting events than any historian or thinker who could have chosen other days.

Faiths could only be judged by hardships rather than victory and winners because anyone can believe when the religion becomes victorious and the associated call prevails, but the soul that truly believes and reflects the true victory of the religion is the one that can steadfast during the hardship and believe while surrounded by all sorts of tribulations.

Accordingly, there is no such date worthier to mark the calendar date than the one when the Prophet departed his home place: "*When the disbelievers drove him out, the second of two, when they (Muhammad and Abu Bakr) were in the cave, and he said to his companion (Abu Bakr): "Be not sad (or afraid), surely Allah is with us." "Then Allah sent down His Sakinah (calmness, tranquility, peace, etc.) upon him, and strengthened him with forces (angels) which you saw not, and made the word of those who disbelieved the lowermost, while it was the Word of Allah that became the uppermost, and Allah is All-Mighty, All-Wise – Quran, 9:40.*""

Let people say that the calendar before and after emigration was known during the time of the Prophet (PBUH), and let them say that entering Madinah is what is meant by the start of the emigration calendar – which is a great day. Let them say this or that, but the date of victory in Quran is clear when it says: "The second of two – Quran, 9:40." And Umar Ibn Al-Khattab was a noble man with an inspired heart, whether he was the one who proposed or accepted [the calendar day], when he considered the 'Cave Thawr[41]' rather than considering the victory day of

[41] Translator: Cave Thawr is where the Prophet and his companion Abu Bakr took shelter to evade Quraysh during their migration from Mecca to Madinah.

Madinah or Battle of Badr, the Battle of Uhod, the Victory in Persia. And he was noble with an inspired heart when he looked at the "*Forces [angles] which you saw not – Quran, 9:40*". And we can see them today [the outcomes of the Angels presence].

The day of calling to Islam was not the first day of Islam, for a call can be made at any time by anyone who can also revoke it after a while or after a bit of time. The birthday of the Prophet was not the first day of Islam, because Muhammad's birth was not an Islamic miracle, unlike Jesus's birth, which is the miracle of Christianity, but Muhammad was a human being like us, who became the master of messengers when he called for Islam, when he saved his mission to where it can survive and flourish, and when its very test occurs in the heart of the caller and his truthful friend, the two [persons] in the cave.

This is how faiths and religions are dated, through hardship rather than through conquests and booties. And it is [the hardship] something in the hearts, so let us recognize it then only in the hearts. And this hardship may be notably unrecognizable, although it is deeply present.

A DAY OF FAITH AND HOPE

The day of the cave is a day of lessons and solaces, especially during the days of anxiety, uncertainty, and anticipation.

It is a day of faith, for it is a day of hope, and a day of contemplating the future by those who are not satisfied with their present and when the present world is not pleasing any of those who care about it. And when the uncertainty and anxiety prevail, be absolutely certain about one particular thing: the world is in search for a spiritual faith! No future can dwell in the hearts unless it attaches to hope and faith. In all human history, no one single great movement was driven by the past that is devoid of a look into the future. On the contrary, all great movements are built on hope in the unseen tomorrow or on goals that can be achieved in human's lifetime with something that can still be achieved in the far tomorrow.

Ali was a young boy in his primary age contemplating the future, and Abu Bakr was an old man leaving life behind him when they both supported Muhammad on the day of Thawr [Emigration]. But they were both knocking at the same door of tomorrow and the same door of hope in which they all agree: the young boy, the old man, and the long-lived who is about to be buried. Because it is the hope of faith, not the hope of the seen moment.

THE FUTURE IS FOR FAITH

What did Islam open for Abu Bakr in life? Did it take him to the past? Or took him to the future? Did it walk him a step forward or brought him a step backward? The truth is that Islam represented the future for the senescence as much as it did for the youth. And it [Islam] detached itself from a volatile state toward a hoped permanent state, and it opened the door of good life for Abu Bakr – not for Ali alone – in this life and the eternal life in the hereafter. And thus is the case with every faith, for it loses the true meaning of faith if all the goodness it brings is confined to something man attain only during his life. Faith must bring about goodness beyond this vanishing life.

Let them remember this fact those who are enthusiastic to advance and lead the future steps, either hastily or slowly; no nation can progress unless it opens the door toward the future and will not look into the past unless it connects with the future. And life will not deliver the future unless it rises newly in the form of a future generation.

Let them remember this those who are confused about a world drowning in its own blood, rejecting its own present, and forsaking its own future. But why are they confused? In seeking the future? In seeking faith? In seeking the reason for man's existence? Because existence alone does not justify, unless we treat humans like animals. Faith is for the future, and let us hope that the future is for faith. And let us hope that the world will always find an everlasting wisdom from the cave day and from the hero of the cave day!

****

CPSIA information can be obtained
at www.ICGtesting.com
Printed in the USA
LVHW011958020821
694317LV00032B/2699

9 780995 382305